When Your Foundations Move

When Your Foundations Move

The Three Crucial Transitions
in Life and Career

C. Michael Thompson

iUniverse, Inc.
Bloomington

WHEN YOUR FOUNDATIONS MOVE
THE THREE CRUCIAL TRANSITIONS IN LIFE AND CAREER

The information, ideas, and suggestions in this book are not intended as a substitute for professional medical advice. Before following any suggestions contained in this book, you should consult your personal physician. Neither the author nor the publisher shall be liable or responsible for any loss or damage allegedly arising as a consequence of your use or application of any information or suggestions in this book.

iUniverse books may be ordered through booksellers or by contacting:

iUniverse
1663 Liberty Drive
Bloomington, IN 47403
www.iuniverse.com
1-800-Authors (1-800-288-4677)

Because of the dynamic nature of the Internet, any web addresses or links contained in this book may have changed since publication and may no longer be valid. The views expressed in this work are solely those of the author and do not necessarily reflect the views of the publisher, and the publisher hereby disclaims any responsibility for them.

Any people depicted in stock imagery provided by Thinkstock are models, and such images are being used for illustrative purposes only.

Certain stock imagery © Thinkstock.

ISBN: 978-1-4759-7639-7 (sc)
ISBN: 978-1-4759-7641-0 (hc)
ISBN: 978-1-4759-7640-3 (e)

Library of Congress Control Number: 2013902810

Printed in the United States of America

iUniverse rev. date: 5/9/2013

To Jane,
through it all

All is flux. Nothing stays still. Nothing endures but change.
—Heraclitus (c. 540–480 BC)

Table of Contents

Introduction xi

The First Shift: Into Your Own 1

The Second Shift: Down at the Crossroads 17

The Third Shift: Leaning into Life 31

Choices I: Work, Jobs, and Career 57

Choices II: Love, Marriage, and Relationships. 81

Mistakes 103

Propellers and Sandbars. 113

Safe Home 135

Your Next Chapter. 153

References. 159

About the Author .169

Introduction

Life must be understood backward. But then one forgets the other clause—that it must be lived forward.
—Soren Kierkegaard, *The Journals*

Now, THAT DOESN'T SEEM quite fair, does it? The famed Danish philosopher is telling us that in this vehicle we call our life, the rear-view mirror works just fine but the headlights are useless. That's like reading the menu after the meal is finished, or the playbill after the curtain falls: it's nice to know what you just experienced, but it would have been a heck of a lot more helpful if you'd had that information beforehand.

This book can offer you that chance.

My career has afforded me the privilege of working closely with current and aspiring leaders in all kinds of organizations—business, government, nonprofits, churches, and the military. I've been able to do that in a variety of roles—as counsel to a large corporation and its executive team, teacher in a leading business school, and, for the last two decades, executive coach and counselor to those tasked with shaping the future of their organizations while attending to their own personal challenges and struggles.

What I have found over the years is less of a discovery than solid confirmation.

- There are predictable transitions—places where the foundations move—in the life and career of every person.
- How those foundational shifts are handled will, in large

measure, determine the success, significance, and satisfaction of that person's career.

- Because our work is so entwined with the rest of our lives, it will have no less dramatic effect on how we come to see the net worth of our larger lives.

So here is this book's offer to you. Your life and career has its own personal and unique storyline. But you may discover within these pages that your story—not unlike those of my clients who've agreed to share their sojourns with you here—has some identifiable, predictable patterns. Perhaps you had a vague sense of that pattern when you were in its throes or knew others who were dealing with similar issues. In the words of T. S. Eliot, you "had the experience but missed the meaning." There is tremendous heuristic value in using that rear-view mirror—understanding backward—and apprehending the lessons that may have been vaguely learned, or totally missed, during that crucial time in your life. Remember that in the old fairy tale, Rumpelstiltskin lost his powers only when he was named.

Or quite possibly, if you have read this far into this introduction, you are in the midst of one of life's crucial transitions right now. This book and its stories will allow you to grasp the meaning behind the experience, giving you some handholds and guideposts along the way and the promise that you can emerge from this foundational shift a far better—if different—person than you were before.

But finally—and this is my fondest hope—you'll get to look at a menu before a plate is plopped in front of you. You can check out the playbill before the production begins. You can make decisions that actively influence the course of your life rather than just watching it unfold from the balcony!

AN OVERVIEW

This book rests upon a foundation that was built by giants. You will hear their names often as you read further. The Swiss psychologist Carl Jung, a one-time student and protégé of Sigmund Freud, provided the substructure upon which much of developmental psychology was built. Eric Erikson, the Pulitzer Prize–winning theorist, was among the first to foray into identifiable stages of life. And Daniel Levinson, through his groundbreaking 1977 work *Seasons of a Man's Life*, directly spawned a number of popular works on the so-called midlife crisis, including Gail Sheehy's several Passages books.

I have no evidence for the old bromide that by standing on the shoulders of giants, you can see farther than they. What I *can* say is that, atop those broad shoulders, I have been able to peer more deeply into the world I know best—organizational life, leadership, and career choices.

Here, in brief overview, is what I've observed:

By some time in our third decade on Earth, we generally find ourselves nicely embedded in a particular work identity. Our jobs have easy descriptions (accountant, lawyer, physician's assistant, manager), and the path for advancement is relatively straightforward. We have role models ahead of us on that path who demonstrate the way. And we are hard on their heels.

The *first* foundational shift will have its roots in the inevitable evolutionary process of becoming one's own person—when we begin to separate from the expectations and assumptions of the cultures, systems (including educational), and family members around us. More importantly, we begin to separate from our *own* expectations and fantasies and discover our real drivers and values—what turns us off and what energizes in our life and work. Depending on when we enter the working world, this period of reevaluation can begin anywhere from our twenties to midthirties. For many it may be, in Levinson's words, more reform than outright revolution. But if this stage is ignored or poorly navigated, it leaves us wholly unprepared for the next seismic shift—the fabled "midlife crisis."

Apart from all the hackneyed stories and jokes, the *second* transition *is* a time of crises and crossroads, where one is presented with an opportunity to redefine—not merely adjust—the foundations of life and career. It is also a time when organizational leaders, as well as the rest of us regular folk, *must* make changes in their existing "formula for success" or risk near-certain career failure in the future. Fortunately, the middle shift is a time when inner resources we never knew we had kick into gear, becoming the "invisible partners" that help us access our hidden strengths, confront our stubborn weaknesses, and expand our personalities. Far more important than sharpening your skills or honing your business acumen, the task of midlife is to grow you as a person.

Somewhere around age fifty, give or take a few years, the foundations will begin a third, more subtle shift that has the power to give a sense of definition and purpose to the remainder of your working life and well beyond. If you have succeeded "well enough" in life's first two crucial transitions (and that's all we should ever ask of ourselves), you are now ready to enter fully into the central tasks of your maturity. Consolidation of what is important to you, rather than continuous expansion for its own sake, now requires the fine art of unpacking and repacking life's luggage—deciding what to leave in and what to leave out.

And yes, in our maturity we experience our own and life's limitations more frontally than before. Yet on the reverse of that same coin we can see our own uniqueness and gifts more clearly and resolve to live them out more authentically than we thought possible in the past. The task, in Erikson's terms, is to choose to live out of our integrity and to eschew despair—to live with our limitations but live out our uniqueness. It is from such lives that lasting legacies come.

THE CHOREOGRAPHY OF LIFE

Each of our three crucial transitions follows a familiar pattern, a kind of choreography of life. Each is preceded by a period of relative stability—an "embeddedness," to borrow Robert Kegan's word—in the norms and structures around us, during which we are content to build upon our existing foundations. But then the shift begins to roll in, perhaps on little cat feet or perhaps with seismic force. During the period of its invasion and occupation of our lives (Levinson thought each transition lasted four to five years), we will at the very least question, reevaluate, and tweak the tenets of our life and career. Some will take the building back to its foundation and start anew.

But at the end of each transition, if all goes "well enough," there is a return to a relative period of stability lasting six to eight years. The outer circumstances of your life may or may not look significantly different than before the transition. But your inner landscape will have significantly changed.

Those who have studied the life cycle in various contexts have observed this same dance from periods of stability to transition and back again. Robert Kegan sees it as the cycle between inclusion and independence, with "evolutionary truces" in between. Psychotherapist

Murray Stein calls it the movement from separation to "liminality" (being on the threshold between two worlds) to reintegration. Robert Kaplan sees the journey moving from the existing "self-system" (being "at home"), to separation ("leaving home"), to an accommodation with the new self ("returning home").

But while each of us has watched that same dynamic unfold in our patients (Stein), research subjects (Levinson, Kegan), and clients (Kaplan, Thompson), none of us can purport to tell the individual reader precisely when these transitions will occur or how long they will last. The exquisite variety of our humanity simply defies our attempts at absolute formulas and chronologies, so the time frames you are offered in this book are rough and approximate. Life, as a colleague of mine puts it, is not "neat."

But it is also true that the challenges and tasks of the twenty-five-year-old are not those of the forty-year-old, which are not those of the fifty-five-year-old. What this book can do is give you a rough map of how lives and careers typically unfold through identifiable stages of development. Its conclusions are drawn from the writings and research on adult development, as well as the hundreds of personal journeys my work has allowed me to observe and share. Rand McNally makes darned good maps, but traveling the road will still be an intensely personal experience.

WHERE'S MY GPS?

In a sense, the issues we are going to confront in these pages are relatively new to the human community. Only in recent generations has the average life expectancy reached a point where we could talk about several distinct life transitions. We also tend to forget that it has only been in the last century or so that business became organized on such a scale, and so engrained in our cultural identity, that we could talk about the effect life changes had on organizational careers.

But most important, Western society has completely discarded the stories, myths, and rituals possessed by practically all early cultures, which helped its members identify and celebrate life's passages. Without such a roadmap, writes James Hollis, "modern individuals are cut adrift to wander without guidance, without models, and without assistance through the various life stages." Thus, life's foundational shifts are "often experienced in frightening and isolating ways, for there are no rites of passage and little help from one's peers who are equally adrift."

It is that sense of isolation, of being adrift with no compass, without handholds or helpmates—confused, divided, or strangely vulnerable— that are the descriptors most often used by those in the throes of a foundational shift. No book can offer the kind of mythic roadmap that was available to earlier cultures. Life is now too complex. Individuals are now, well, too individual. But here's betting that in these pages you'll be able to see your own map more clearly, along with that big red "X" that says "You Are Here." Just as important, you'll see that you have plenty of company.

It is cold comfort to hear Dr. Jung say, "I [have] learned that the greatest and most important problems of life are fundamentally insoluble. ... They can never be solved, but only outgrown." But the truth is that if there is no "outgrowing" in time—no adequate resolution of a particular foundational shift—then almost by definition more unresolved issues will be taken into the next phase of life, and the next shift will be all the more disquieting. Or worse.

It is a difficult thing for a bird to be hatched out of the relative safety of its shell and more difficult still for it to learn to fly to new habitats and strange climes. But we all know what happens to eggs that don't hatch and birds that can't fly.

The First Shift:
Into Your Own

But the meaning of life is not exhaustively explained by your business activities, nor is the deep desire of the human heart answered by your bank account, even if you have never heard of anything else.
—Carl Jung

The greatest derangement of the mind is to believe in something because we wish it to be so.
—Louis Pasteur

TAYLOR GATTIS WAS ON the path. Better put, she was on trajectory. As if shot from a cannon, she had blown through the best education her parents could provide, from the "right" kindergarten to the classy gated college to the prestigious MBA program. And in between there had been all the accoutrements necessary to produce a finished product her parents could be proud of: flute lessons, soccer camp, study abroad, the occasional tutor when needed.

And now, barely thirty-one, Taylor could reap the benefits of their investment and her own hard work. She was an account representative for a Fortune 500 company, fast-tracked for a management role, and a star that seemed to be rising in step with her trajectory.

"There was never any question what I would do after college," she said. "It wasn't a decision so much as an assumption. I'm not sure I ever really thought about it, certainly not to the extent of considering alternatives. Dad had made a good career in business and mom had sacrificed some of her own interests to support that. I was smart and always pretty much the 'good kid' who enjoyed pleasing them, and that was that."

But Taylor wasn't in my office to tell me how well things were going. The bureaucracy and politics of a large corporation were starting to get her down, and the brutal travel schedule was taking its toll. "Mom says all I need is a 'fella,' but I don't think I'm capable of making anybody else happy right now, until I'm a lot happier myself."

And what would that take? "I don't know. I feel ... strangely divided. It's like there's this part of me that really enjoys the work and camaraderie and travel and absolute thrill of nailing a deal; and I feel lucky to be making the kind of money I make at my age. But the bloom's coming off the rose. There's this other part of me that misses having the time to dig in the flower garden—misses not *having* a flower garden—and wonders, *How much longer can I do this?* I'm scared that at this pace I'll never have the life and family I've always wanted, but I'm *terrified* of what I'll lose if I leave.

"And besides all that, what will my parents think?"

NOVICE ADULTHOOD

"Inertia" seems like a dirty word, doesn't it? We associate it with all things sluggish, stuck, lazy. We forget that its meaning encompasses not only the tendency of inert objects to remain at rest but the way matter keeps moving in the same straight line until acted upon by some external force. Such was the trajectory of Taylor Gattis's path, as it is with most people in their twenties and early thirties. Spurred by both a burning desire to succeed and a yawning fear of failure, they attack novice adulthood with a zeal and physical vigor that will rarely be replicated in their lives. Onward and ever upward!

There is indeed much to be done: establishing oneself at work, sifting through love relationships, building a physical space apart from previous family and community, finding a circle of trusted friends. "Hire me, marry me, trust me," he or she might be heard to say, "and then let me prove myself worthy." Promotions, credentials, recognition, self-confidence, and a sense of "making it" in the world become vitally important, followed closely by the sense of identity that comes from establishing a new nuclear family, becoming embedded in a community of friends and colleagues, and having one's own "lifestyle."

And all of these efforts are vital parts of the "project" of establishing a foothold in the world. If we were to relate it to the old myths and stories of our culture, we would talk about this time of life as being an initiation, or rite of passage, from the insular world of our youth to the independence and concomitant responsibilities of adulthood. In one way or another, each of us "goes off to the wars" and are forced into forms of self-reliance that most of us (fortunately) did not have to know before.

The forward inertia of the young adult provides the sheer will and energy to complete the task of establishing one's place in the world. This is no mean accomplishment, and society itself would cease to flourish if this were not the natural flow of life. But just as the summer solstice begins the shortened days of the winter to come, that forward energy contains within it the very factors that will eventually slow or bring it to a grinding halt. These are the factors—as much a part of life's flow as the trajectory itself—that may shake the foundations of the project to which you have devoted yourself so earnestly.

Consider Taylor Gattis. She may have achieved more than most in her thirty-one years, but like everyone else she entered novice adulthood with a set of values, expectations, and assumptions that were imported from an earlier time and place. And she, like practically all other young adults, was as unaware of the borrowed nature of those assumptions as a fish is aware that it swims in water. "I'm not sure I ever really thought about it," said she.

"No one can take the step into life without making certain assumptions," Jung observed, "and occasionally those assumptions are false—that is, they do not fit the conditions into which one is thrown." This is the stuff of the first foundational shift. It may begin with a nagging feeling of discontent, a dissonance between what is experiencing in day to day life and some "little voice within" that keeps implying that all is not as well as you had assumed it would be. There's a mismatch, though one is hard-pressed to put words to what is mismatched.

Here's how writer and educator Parker Palmer described what that feeling was like for him:

I was in my early thirties when I began, literally, to wake up to questions about my vocation. By all appearances, things were going well, but the soul does not put much stock in appearances. Seeking a path more purposeful than accumulating wealth, holding power, winning at competition, or securing a career, I had started to understand that it is indeed possible to live a life other than one's own. Fearful that I was doing just that—but uncertain about the deeper, truer life I sensed hidden inside me, uncertain whether it was real or trustworthy or within reach—I would snap awake in the middle of the night and stare for long hours at the ceiling.

With a bit of good fortune we can at least arrive at the place Parker Palmer (and eventually Taylor Gattis) did. We can realize that our lives so far have been based on certain assumptions, and we can evaluate whether those assumptions are serving us well. We can realize that part of what's been driving our bus are the accumulated expectations of family members, teachers, friends, significant others—and, of course, ourselves—and take a studied look at where the bus is now headed. And we can hold up to the light our inherited values and see if they are truly golden or merely glisten.

Writing three decades after the experiences recounted above, Palmer had this advice: "Before you tell your life what you intend to do with it, listen for what it intends to do with you. Before you tell your life what truths and values you have decided to live up to, let your life tell you what truths you embody, what values you represent." In short, come into your own.

Pathways

While the movements that take place in a person's heart and mind are not always overtly visible even to family and friends, experience tells us the first great foundational shift takes one of three recognizable forms.

The first is the experience of those fortunate (?) few whose inherited expectations, values, and assumptions are a relative match for "the conditions into which one is thrown." Their transition from the educational and family systems to novice adulthood is relatively smooth, without overt disruption or a need for fundamental reevaluation and change.

But there is great danger in thinking that statement applies to you. First, Levinson's research is clear that this happy situation applies to a distinct *minority* of young adults. Remember, it is as difficult as it is courageous to objectively examine your own assumptions and expectations to determine if they are truly owned or merely borrowed. One loses a piece of their potentiality—a chunk of their future—by concluding without honest reflection that their assumptions about life are spot-on. Still, we all know people for whom the twenties and thirties seem to be an effortless transition.

The trouble is, this minority closely resembles from the outside a far larger group who are in active and open *resistance* to anything that would threaten to interrupt their forward inertia, or have found the shut-off switch for that irritating "little voice within." There's just too much at stake—simply too much to lose—to warrant an examination of one's life and direction. It is far easier to dismiss those inner rumblings as "just a phase" or as some sort of mental indigestion which given time and a couple of pills (or drinks) will dissipate.

As the poet T. S. Eliot characterizes it, "Distracted from distraction by distraction/Filled with fancies and empty of meaning," this second common way of dealing with life's fundamental shift is hard to spot because we wish to keep it a secret even from ourselves. We use the zeal and energy which powered the project in the first place to extend it uninterrupted into the indefinite future.

And the drivers behind this strategy for dealing with life are understandably self-protective. As Levinson sympathetically observed, "Every genuine reappraisal must be agonizing, because it challenges the illusions and vested interests upon which the existing structure is based. The life structure of the thirties was initiated and stabilized by powerful forces in the person and his environment. These forces continue to make their claim for preserving the status quo."

But as we will see, it is those who resist dealing with the first foundational shift at all that have the greatest difficulties with the second—the one we call midlife.

CHARLES

There is a third path. Not surprisingly, since life seems to be structured this way, that path is both the most conscious and the most uncomfortable. The author Pearl S. Buck put it nicely: "It is no simple matter to pause in the midst of one's maturity, when life is full of function, to examine what are the principles which control that functioning." And yet, as Oliver Wendell Holmes asserted, "To have doubted one's own first principles is the mark of a civilized man."

Sometimes, as was the case with Taylor Gattis, we pause and engage in conscious self-reflection because the inner dissonance becomes so loud that we can hardly do otherwise. Such people, in Jung's words, become unable to "content themselves with inadequate or wrong reasons to the questions of life." Often instead it comes as the result of some precipitating event—a failed relationship, problems at work, an accident or illness—that becomes the external force that knocks us off our straight line trajectory.

Such was the case with a client I'll call Charles. Armed with an undergraduate degree in criminal justice and a diploma from a good law school, he embarked upon his chosen profession as an associate in a large law firm. He had taken this position with his eyes wide open—he knew there would be one sharp learning curve after another, that it would take sixty to seventy hours a week to meet the firm's expectations for billable hours, and that it would be six to seven years at a minimum before he would be offered partnership in the firm.

But when the time finally came for Charles to be considered for the brass ring of partnership, he was told that primarily as a result of a misstep in handling a client matter earlier in his career, a decision on his candidacy had been deferred for at least another year. Having put all his emotional eggs into this one basket, Charles was understandably deflated and depressed. To make matters worse, in pursuit of the partnership prize he had neglected a long-term romantic relationship that now seemed to be hanging by a thread, and a long-postponed physical revealed a form of hypertension related to stress.

Seemingly not able to summon his signature resilience to just "plow through" his current situation, Charles took a step back. He began to think about—and put words around—the reasons he'd gone to law school in the first place. He reflected back on the courses that had enlivened him as an undergraduate and why he had chosen criminal justice as a major. "As corny as this sounds, I've always been fascinated by our judicial system, warts and all, and wanted to be a part of it. I saw myself as Elliot Stabler [of TV's *Law and Order*] or a modern-day Eliot Ness, laying myself out there to make small dents in big societal problems."

So what happened? "Law school and firm practice were just sitting there as obvious choices. I mean, my parents were supportive, many of my classmates considered it a logical next step—and then I knocked the top off the LSATs and that was that. Look, I wouldn't give anything for what I learned practicing law, and I wouldn't begrudge anyone else that life, but I went into it assuming it would be something it could never be for me. If I'd stayed, it would have wrecked my life."

His life—not the one chosen by circumstance or convenience or family or classmates—but the one he wished to claim as his own. So after dealing with his disappointment and giving himself permission to step back and examine his career choice, Charles devised a long-term exit strategy that would allow him to keep his well-compensated position while exploring other options. Through an old college professor, Charles landed an interview with the FBI, which was interested in a person with his background and skills. He and his girlfriend openly discussed the pros and cons of such a dramatic move—certainly less money but more reasonable hours, more personal satisfaction, and more interesting travel. As he brought her more into the decision process, the relationship between them deepened.

As so often happens in the midst of such reexaminations, Charles began to feel a pull back toward the religious convictions of his youth and began to reread scriptural passages that had been important in his formative years. "I hadn't been to church, outside of the occasional wedding, since high school. But the passages that really spoke to me had to do with service and justice and sacrifice for a higher good. I'm no religious nut—or a political one—but it's interesting how the values that stuck with me as a kid made full circle and came back to me as a grown man."

Charles was indeed offered partnership by the firm one year after his initial rebuff. He turned it down and instead accepted a position with significant responsibilities in an FBI regional office—and got married to boot. During this decisive year, he also found for himself a spiritual community that helped affirm the values that had come to greater prominence in his life and had served as a basis for his career move.

Charles sums it up this way: "I feel like, in a way, I flew blind through college and law school and right into my first job. In hindsight, not making partner on my predetermined timeline was the best thing that could have happened to me. I had to take a hard look at who I really was and what I really wanted. And again, I know this sounds corny, but there's just always been this persistent dream of contributing to society by being part of the best criminal justice system the world has yet devised. I liked saying I was a lawyer because it had a certain social status attached to it. I like saying I'm with the Federal Bureau of Investigation because it speaks more of who I really am."

CHARLOTTE

With "Charlotte," the changes wrought by the first foundational shift took place somewhat later chronologically and were less obvious to the beholder, but they were no less transformational to her life. Charlotte always described herself, with more pride than apology, as being "from the other side of the tracks." And she did what most young women in her community did upon graduating from high school—got married and promptly had children. But Charlotte knew she was bright enough to continue her education, and with the encouragement of a devoted mother (who was also an excellent babysitter), she set her sights on two distinct goals: a college degree in accounting and a job with a "big four" accounting firm.

By age thirty-four, both goals had been accomplished, yet they failed to bring the sense of contentment she had assumed they would. Charlotte's position required a fair amount of travel, and the nature of the client work often entailed long and irregular hours. Her children were well cared for, but she simply missed them, and no amount of treats and stuffed animals from distant airports could make them miss her less. Even her relationship with her husband, who was a good man and supportive partner through Charlotte's long quest to fulfill her goals, was showing signs of withering after years of a piecemeal family life and part-time marriage.

In her own words: "Ambition is a good thing. It got me out of the zip code I was born in and got me an education and opportunities I'd never have had otherwise. But when is enough, enough? When do you realize that the eagle has already landed? I set out to prove I wasn't just another girl from 'shack town,' and I did that. But I was carrying around some myth that said that if I jumped through this hoop, and then this one, and then this one, I'd win the 'happiness for life' lottery or something. It doesn't work like that. Life is more about cycles than straight lines."

It took almost two years and the cooperation of an employer who really wanted to keep her, but Charlotte reinvented herself within the firm and reinvigorated her life outside it. She moved laterally to a different functional area where her skill at strategic planning could supplant her client-facing duties and reduce her travel schedule. She took advantage of the firm's telecommuting policy to work from home two days a week. Her husband, who had himself achieved a degree in architecture, designed and built a home they adored.

"For me," says Charlotte, "it was all about stepping back and realizing that just continuing to plow ahead was not going to get me what I needed in the long term. It wasn't going to be good for my marriage or my children, obviously, but the big breakthrough was in realizing it wasn't what I wanted out of life. I let a number of ideas and possibilities incubate and gave them some time, without feeling like I had to jump on one of them right away. It was far from being easy and involved taking some risks, but I'm honestly like a different person now. I'm happier, and"—she says with a chuckle—"I'm actually better compensated than I ever thought I'd be. Life's good!"

NEEDFUL VIRTUES

The key here seems to be in the "pulling back," whether we do so consciously and willingly (as did Charlotte) or whether we are forced into it by outer occurrences (a la Charles). We create for ourselves a kind of objective perch from which to view our own lives. We can use that perspective to examine, in Pearl S. Buck's language, the principles that control our lives and functioning. Most importantly, we can discern whether those principles are self-chosen and will serve our highest good going forward.

In addition to this skill of self-reflection—the ability to take a third-party perspective upon your own life story—two other virtues are necessary.

One is patience. Notice it took Charles a year and Charlotte almost two before the inner and outer changes wrought by the first foundational shift fully took root in their lives. Just as you place yourself at peril by ignoring or postponing life's flow, you are equally ill-served by trying to push the river—attempting to treat it with the same left-brain urgency as the month-end financials or that report due in two weeks. Find for yourself a place of patience, which is neither a dull lethargy nor an obsessive scramble, but admits of an understanding that most good things in life grow incrementally and over time.

Yet the most essential virtue may be the willingness and ability to take a risk. After all, no one likes change but a wet baby. But Erik Erikson states the challenge unequivocally in this way: "The strength acquired at any stage is tested by the necessity to transcend it in such a way that the individual can take chances in the next stage with what was most vulnerably precious in the previous one." In other words, what we valued most in an earlier phase of life—what most defined us—has to undergo the risks that self-examination entails in order for growth in the next phase to occur.

You can bet your calculator that earlier in her career, Charlotte wouldn't have risked *anything* "lateral" as a newly minted accountant in dogged pursuit of advancement in the firm's hierarchy. Charles had to risk social and financial status. Taylor was "terrified' of what she stood to lose and wondered if her parents might disapprove. Such are examples of the risks inherent in coming into one's own.

The psychotherapist James Hollis tells the true story of a man in this time of life who failed at both self-reflection and patience. At the age of twenty-eight, he had already achieved the goals he had inherited from his educational and family systems. He had a PhD, had published a book, had started a family, and enjoyed a good university teaching position. A good many years later, when he looked back on that time in his life, he was able to recall that he was starting to lose his forward energy and feel a sense of boredom.

His solution: simply try harder to do more of the same. Over the next decade he wrote more, had more children, and taught at ever-better posts at higher-ranked universities. When he was thirty-seven he fell into a full-blown depression, complete with a total loss of energy for the things of the outer world, and a loss of meaning within. He quit his job, left his family, and opened an ice cream parlor.

I didn't know this man, but I do know many who would resemble him, to one degree or another. They may not be former college professors serving up banana splits, but in their "lives of quiet desperation," they have failed or refused the task of self-reflection given to this time of life, or they have impatiently bounced from pillar to post, never finding what they seek. Or, as in Dr. Hollis's example, they have taken a foolhardy and unnecessary risk born of pent-up years of frustration. There is a better way.

TAYLOR REVISITED

Seismologists tell us the most violent and visible of our earthquakes occur when the natural movement of the earth's plates against one another becomes impeded or stuck, resulting in cataclysmic upheaval when the pressure is finally released. But the earth actually experiences as many as a million "silent" earthquakes every year. The tectonic plates separate, collide, and slide past each other without major incident.

Within the earth itself, as on its surface, constant change, movement, and friction is the norm. The true danger lies in getting stuck.

Which brings us back to Taylor Gattis. Two years after that first meeting in my office, much had changed about her life. But even to her family, those changes seemed more like a natural evolution than a seismic shift. Only a few of her closest friends—and I as her coach— knew how much reflection, patience, and risk-taking had gone into this time. And the payoff was truly exceptional.

Taylor began by admitting to herself that she was giving more to her then-current job than she was getting in return. "The first internal myth I had to debunk," she said, "was that if I tried really hard to love my job, it would love me back. I'm not sure where I got that idea, but it certainly wasn't realistic. No job or company can meet that internal need for you."

So she began a "soft search" within her city, looking for smaller companies with less geographic reach that needed the transferable skills she could bring to the table. "I surprised myself. I had three really good offers within the first three months." Taylor now manages a small group of professionals, which include marketing staff as well as sales reps. "That's gotten me stretched out of the narrow sales role I had with my previous company and opened up a whole new area of knowledge and experience."

Her lighter travel schedule has freed up more time for friends and family but also had the unintended consequence of leaving space for a "fella" to barge his way into her life. At this writing, they are engaged and talking about wedding dates.

And what about the flower garden? Taylor has moved from the high-rise apartment near her downtown office to a suburban townhouse, complete with a small garden. "I had no idea how much this really meant to me until I got back to tending flowers. It's a huge release and somehow taps something creative in me. And it's hard not to feel grounded and connected to the things around you when you're up to your elbows in cow manure."

Hers is a deep, genuine laugh I never would have heard two years earlier.

Does Gender or Generation Matter?

You have noticed that many of the examples I have used in this chapter are women. That was intentional. Levinson's conclusions were thought suspect because his original subjects were all males, and Erikson and Jung (as was the custom of their times) wrote primarily in the masculine. But does one's gender affect the foundational shifts we are discussing here? The answer is an unequivocal yes and no.

It has been my experience that the seismic forces we are examining in this book occur within both men and women. Moreover, it has been my consistent observation that the more oriented toward business their educational background and the more they find themselves in traditional hierarchical business environments, the less differences between men and women I can see.

What *does* often differ are the ways in which those life changes are experienced, and the types of choices typically made. Women are *somewhat* more likely to choose to begin a family and postpone higher education and career (as did Charlotte), and they are also more likely to make adjustments in the first foundational shift based on the value they place on family and relationships. Women often are—and give themselves permission to be—more reflective than their male counterparts and more patient with the pace of change. The extent to which such differences have a hormonal basis is a subject of current discussion and debate, but it is undeniably true that women have more estrogen and serotonin, which together can heighten the desire for harmony, connection, and calmness.

The male of the species, through genetics or acculturation or both, is somewhat better at taking risks and less concerned about the views of parental figures, owing perhaps in part to the fact that they are possessed of up to one hundred times more testosterone, that fast-acting hormone that fuels aggression, competitiveness, and risky behavior.

All of the foregoing statements are generalizations, of course, for which there are many exceptions. But it is certainly true that being a man or a woman will color your experience of the first foundational shift and help shape your responses to it.

But what about your "generation"? Sociologists have studied with some fascination in recent years the differences in shared values between the so-called baby boomers (those born between 1946 and 1964) and generation X (born between 1965 and 1982). While the former would place a high value on loyalty, competitive achievement, and "paying your dues" to move up the corporate hierarchy, the latter would be more characterized by impatience, entrepreneurial independence, and work-family balance.

So one might imagine a conversation between Taylor and her parents that would go something like this:

Mom: Sweetheart, you know we only want what's best for you.

Taylor: Then I know you'll support me in making this change. I really think it's the best thing for me.

Dad: Have you thought through what you'll be giving up? You're proving yourself on a big time stage here. You'll be getting stock options soon.

Taylor: I don't need a company with international name recognition to enjoy what I do.

Mom: But haven't they invested a lot of time and money in bringing you along? Don't you feel like you owe them something for the faith they've put in you?

Taylor: Mom, you know that people change jobs and even careers multiple times these days. It's not at all unexpected and they understand my reasons.

Dad: We just want you to have the security we've enjoyed, that's all. What if this company goes belly up? I've never even heard of them!

Taylor (getting a bit exasperated): Then I'll take what I've learned to another company! And how secure is the Fortune 100 these days? Who was forced to take a package long before they wanted to retire—not to mention they're now monkeying around with your retirement plan and health-care coverage!

Dad: Your mother and I just felt like you were on the verge of hitting it big.

Taylor: I was on the verge of burning myself to the ground. *Now* I'm on the verge of hitting it big—in my own way and on my own terms. Besides, I've got a wedding to plan!

We often use the word *integrity* to connote adherence to a particular moral framework or code of conduct. When I think about Taylor these days, I am drawn more of the original Latin meaning of the word "integrity": *whole, entire, intact, undivided.* It's the same concept we apply today to mathematical "whole numbers" that express a unique and undivided quantity.

She, like Charles and Charlotte, found their own individual identities during this time of life, shedding preconceived and restrictive cocoons as they went, until they were able to put their own personal stamps upon their lives and careers. They no longer felt "strangely divided," to recall Taylor's words. This is integrity, not from following codes or expectations or wishes from without, but from heeding that "little voice within." It is integrity in depth, an important consequence of the first foundational shift.

As generation Y—the "millennial generation"—encounters the time of this first foundational shift, it will be interesting to see how their particular admixture of multiculturalism, desire for challenging and creative work, need for praise, and disdain for being micromanaged helps mold their decisions about life and career in young adulthood. The only certainty is that it will.

Every succeeding generation will have its own shared set of values and experiences that will shape its identity, yet the underlying choreography of life will go on. The Gen-Yers will continue to graduate from their family and other adolescent structures years after they've graduated from high school or college. The first foundational shift will continue to shake and reshape their lives. We can only imagine what Taylor's conversation with her own children will sound like.

The Second Shift:
Down at the Crossroads

The nearer we approach to the middle of life, and the better we have succeeded in entrenching ourselves in our personal attitudes and social positions, the more it appears as if we had discovered the right course and the right ideals and principles of behaviour. For this reason we suppose them to be eternally valid, and make a virtue of unchangeably clinging to them ... But we cannot live the afternoon of life according to the programme of life's morning; for what was great in the morning will be little at evening, and what in the morning was true will at evening have become a lie.—Carl Jung

The afternoon knows what the morning never suspected.—Swedish Proverb

As the choreography of life continues after the first foundational shift, most men and women enter a period of settling down and settling into the choices they have made for themselves. Like the character Harold Cooper (played by Kevin Kline) in the classic movie *The Big Chill*, we can exclaim, "I'm dug in here." We have established a place for ourselves at work, in our communities, and within our families.

In addition to striking roots deeply into the ground, the image of a ladder often resonates with us as well. We increase "rung by rung" our income, our social standing, and our sense of "making it" in the world as our own person. We have our plans for the future and specific timetables for getting there—e.g., vacation home by thirty-seven, vice president by forty, financial independence by fifty. Put a bit more negatively, it is the all-out pursuit of what William James calls the "bitch-goddess success." Life seems pretty straightforward—the movement is straight and the direction is ever forward.

But as we have already discovered, life seems to abhor a straight line. Enter, stage left, the second foundational shift.

Many popular works on the so-called midlife crisis open with these lines from Dante's *Divine Comedy*:

"Midway this way of life we're bound upon,
I wake to find myself in a dark wood,
Where the right road was wholly lost and gone."
(Translation by Dorothy Sayers)

Something about these lines seems to encapsulate the feeling that often overtakes us in our middle years. Suddenly, it seems, the path doesn't seem quite so straight and the way "forward" has become less than clear.

Using the analogy of the sun's daily path, Jung thought he observed a "deep-seated and peculiar change in the psyche" around the "noontime of life," which he believed commonly occurred in his patients between the ages of thirty-five and forty. Jung believed the transition from morning to afternoon would rarely be seamless or steady. At one extreme, he saw that it could be a "dangerous age" giving rise to "changes of profession, divorces, religious convulsions [and] apostasies of every description." On the other hand, the shift might be less obvious to the individual and those around him, "like a slow change in a person's character." Jung noticed that in certain of his patients, traits began to subtly surface that had disappeared since childhood, while strong inclinations and interests would begin to weaken and others take their place.

But whatever the course, from *sturm und drang* to slow and subtle change, Jung is clear about the consequences of *not* navigating the midlife transition: "Conversely—and this happens very frequently— one's cherished convictions and principles ... begin to harden and grow increasingly rigid until, somewhere around the age of fifty, a period of intolerance and fanaticism is reached. It is as if the existence of these principles were endangered and it were therefore necessary to emphasize them all the more."

While Jung made reference to particular chronological ages, midlife is more a developmental (and some would say spiritual) process than a chronological one. In fact, there is credible evidence that the shift-point described by Jung has, for a great many modern people, been stretched out five to ten years or more. What Jung may have observed in his patients at around the age of forty, I am just as likely to see in my modern coaching clients anywhere between the ages of thirty-five and fifty-five, depending on a variety of factors affecting their personal developmental path.

MIDLIFE MALAISE

While we can be sure the midlife transition *does* happen, *why* does it happen? Let's see if we can spot what is hiding under the words of two of my coaching clients, Steve Conroy and Olivia Drews.

Steve, the forty-two-year-old director of a non-profit agency, sits behind his desk and wonders where his trademark zest and enthusiasm have gone. "I just don't feel like myself," he confides. "Seems like over the past couple of years all the color has just drained out of this job for me. What felt for so long like love of my work now just feels like dull-as-dirt duty. Some days I just don't feel like getting up—and you know that's not like me." He asks, "How do I keep my staff motivated for the important stuff we do here if I can't even motivate myself?"

Olivia, just six months after her "dream promotion" to vice president, now questions the very career choice that she has so successfully pursued. "I'll tell you a secret: I don't know that I can keep this up until retirement," she says, "and that's ten, maybe fifteen years away. The pressure to do ever more with always less is unrelenting. It's hard to find any sort of break, and I feel guilty that I'm shortchanging my husband and kids. Sometimes I wonder if there shouldn't be more to life than there is—and I'm not getting any younger!"

Neither Steve nor Olivia had much clarity about the causes of what they were feeling, much less what to do about it. But they shared many symptoms with others during this critical time of life: a vague sense of malaise, a feeling of stagnation or boredom, even a certain hopelessness as they surveyed the future and could only see "more of the same."

Catherine Fitzgerald, in her research on personality development of managers at midlife, talks about a descending sense of real sadness:

> Some have attributed this sadness to an awareness of death, but that interpretation is not consistent with my discussions with people who are going through the process. The sadness seems to come from two related feelings. One feeling is that something important is missing in life, that what was fine until fairly recently is no longer satisfying. Exactly what is missing and how to obtain [it] are extremely unclear to the person experiencing the process. The second feeling involves a sense that "I've worked so hard to develop myself and create my life, why all of a sudden is it not good enough?"

There is an underlying psychology of midlife that can help us understand why Steve and Olivia are feeling as they do. Beneath the typical inner symptoms (boredom, depression, anxiety, lack of fulfillment, etc.) and the outer, visible events (such as job or partner changes, substance abuse, infidelity), there lie some fundamental truths. Those tectonic plates shifting within us have become snagged yet again, and that force welling up within us can be felt either vaguely or oppressively. When it is consciously recognized and acknowledged, it can cause everything from mild anxiety to a sense that one's direction has been "wholly lost." When it is unrecognized or repressed, it will present itself as a depressive sadness, as if our lifeblood itself had lost its natural flow. We can experience anything from a loss of energy for things (or people) that used to bring us joy, all the way to thoughts of suicide.

To make matters worse, says James Hollis, we will almost always continue to repeat the old patterns and behaviors that used to keep these feelings at bay with ever increasing urgency (that is, compulsion), but ever-decreasing effectiveness.

> Changing one's job or relationship does not change one's sense of oneself over the long run. When increasing pressure from within becomes less and less containable by the old strategy, a crisis of selfhood erupts. We do not know who we are, really,

apart from social roles and psychic reflexes. And we do not know what to do to lessen the pressure.

There sometimes is, but need not be, a "marker event" that brings on the midlife transition, such as a job loss, divorce, or illness. For most, the pressures within us simply achieve critical mass. In fact, it's been my experience that those "marker events" are more the *result* of a midlife crisis than they are its cause.

THE PARADOX OF IDENTITY

But this question remains: Why do the tectonic plates get stuck, yet again, at this noontime of life? Why does the choreography shift on us when things were going so doggone well?

The reason for this dastardly turn of events has to do with what Robert A. Johnson calls the "paradox of identity." We spend much of the first half of our lives, *as we should*, defining and refining ourselves. We have an ego—an "I"—that gives us our particular place in the world. In the first foundational shift of our adult lives, we may actually be called upon to wrest part of that identity away from others' expectations. We stake our claim to those features that are truly "I," and we dismiss those that aren't.

Me at that age? "I" was a lawyer. I was a teacher. I was a husband, new father, and pretty fair body surfer. I was active in the church and community. I was a spiritual seeker. I made my parents proud. Those were some of the ways, on the positive side of the coin, I defined myself. But as that same Robert Johnson (whom I was blessed to have as a mentor) helped me learn, I was so closely identified with this "I" that I came to think it was the sum total of who I was. And it became very difficult to change once life began to demand that of me.

Johnson says, "We do our best to catch hold of life by acting as if it is stable and unchanging. We seek structure, form, and meaning, and then we become limited by our structures, forms, and meanings. In truth, the ego with which we identify is an accumulation of old habits conditioned by past experience and held together by the paper clips and chewing gum of memory. It does its best to make our experience safe and predictable, but it can also inhibit us. This is the paradox of identity."

If life is change (and believe me on this one, it is), then the "structures, forms, and meanings" that make up our "I" will *inevitably* fail to serve us for the indefinite term. And that is both good and necessary. Again, Jung:

> The significance of the morning undoubtedly lies in the development of the individual, our entrenchment in the outer world, the propagation of our kind, and the care of our children. This is the obvious purpose of nature. But when this purpose has been attained—and more than attained—shall the earning of money, the extension of conquests, and the expansion of life go steadily on beyond the bounds of all reason and sense? Whoever carries over into the afternoon the law of the morning, or the natural aim, must pay for it with damage to his soul, just as surely as a growing youth who tries to carry over his childish egoism into adult life must pay for this mistake with social failure.

But let's look at this transition from something of an opposite direction for a moment. If it is truly part of life's flow—made necessary by the paradox of identity and the pressure that builds from the resulting "stuck plates"—is the inevitable result only angst and misery for all the years the transition may last? Far from it. As we will see as this book unfolds, that characteristic loss of energy can give way to new invigoration as life's flow finds a new gradient. Anxiety can give way to a sense of immediacy, playfulness, and living in the present. Some in the throes of the midlife transition describe having their first "ecstatic" (which means, literally, to stand outside oneself) experience while others discover a long-forgotten spirituality.

Levinson found much the same in his research. "For these men, middle adulthood is often the fullest and most creative season in the life cycle. They are less tyrannized by the ambitions, passions, and illusions of youth. They can be more deeply attached to others and yet more separate, more centered in the self. For them, the season passes in its best and most satisfying rhythm."

"Truth" in the Afternoon of Life

The morning—life's first half—focused on the building of a family, a career, and a place in the outer world. It was about adapting, finding one's niche, and, for everyone to some extent, conforming. It involved choosing roles and relationships, grabbing a ladder, and deciding which wall to set it against. It was a time for revisiting and often revising our priorities. And very importantly, it was about wresting one's own personal values and purposes from the web of family and other relationships.

What then of the afternoon of life? What happens when we have consolidated our physical existence, struck our roots into the world, and come into our own as adults? Here is where the difficulty begins. We have, perhaps only ten years before as part of our first foundational shift, examined our values and goals to see if they truly spoke of us as individuals. Now, in the second shift, we are entering a time of life that calls for us to do more than just break away from infantile ties and illusions. It calls upon us to reexamine *everything*.

> The transition from morning to afternoon means a revaluation of the earlier values. There comes the urgent need to appreciate the value of the opposite of our former ideals, to perceive the error in our former convictions, to recognize the untruth in our former truth, and to feel how much antagonism and even hatred lay in what, until now, had passed for love.

These words from Jung are strong and disturbing. Why should such a thing be necessary? Because our own "truths" can keep us bound and stuck in the developmental place where we now stand. Because just as we seek "structure, form, and meaning" and then become limited by those same structures, forms, and meanings, a truth too heavily clung to can become a ball and chain around one's midlife foot.

Spanish philosopher José Ortega y Gasset said it with characteristic eloquence: "Our firmest convictions are apt to be the most suspect. They mark our limitations and our bounds. Life is a petty thing unless it is moved by the indomitable urge to extend its boundaries."

It is not that our convictions, morals, and life principles suddenly become wrong-headed. To the contrary, they can remain beacons for us in a time of personal turmoil. But it may be important, for midlife growth to occur, for us to examine those truths upon which we have based our past decisions and acknowledge that even their opposite may contain some truth. It may be important, in examining the rules by which we have lived, to acknowledge that there are very few rules that are generalizable for all situations under all circumstances and for all people. Without some appreciation for contradiction and paradox that neither threatens us nor sends us clamoring for resolution at all cost, we will always be looking for that one right either/or answer.

And the dynamics of midlife will, if nothing else, disabuse us of the notion that there is always one right, either/or answer that is consistent with our own historical values and priorities. How else could a person with a lifelong focus on "winning" competitively at all cost come to terms with unfair corporate politics that blocks his or her advancement? A deep commitment to loyalty looks very different when it is up to you to decide which trusted subordinate to lay off. And your trust in absolute fidelity might be tested when your spouse tells you she's had a brief affair but now wants to make it right.

Not that those values now flip to their opposites. But doggedly clinging to a narrow version of them can cost you your job, your self-respect, or your marriage. Such is the stuff of reevaluation at midlife.

OUR FORMULA FOR SUCCESS

At the Bolger Center for Leadership Development in Potomac, Maryland, four senior officers of the US Postal Service were seated around a table, silently digesting the written feedback they had just received from their coworkers. I had already seen the feedback and was keenly watching for their reactions. One by one the faces fell and the frowns appeared. They were reading words and phrases that included "autocratic," "arrogant," "impatient," "insensitive," "aloof," and "his way or the highway."

Then, as corporate trainers are wont to do, we asked these highly placed and heretofore successful executives to talk about their feedback among themselves. Said one, "I got this job because I'm direct, I get results, and I take no prisoners. Now, how is it all of a sudden that I'm 'too aggressive'? What in the world does that mean?" Said another, "And what's this about de-motivating my people? How the hell can they not be motivated if we're fighting for financial survival out there?"

But then, over the course of the next hour, something happened that no trainer could orchestrate and no lecture could accomplish: they *got it*. When asked at the end of their discussion to display their mutual conclusions on a flipchart, here are two things they wrote:

"The traits that got us here are the very traits we now need to curtail or control," and

"Ironically, the same traits that made/make us successful now have the potential to make us unsuccessful!"

I doubt any of those gentlemen knew of Charles Handy, that Irish sage of the business press, but not even he was more spot-on when he observed, "It is one of the paradoxes of success that the things and ways that got you there are seldom those things that keep you there."

This is not some cruel trick of the universe. It is simply part and parcel of the second foundational shift that we call midlife. And never is it more apparent than in the lives and careers of people in business and other organizations. So the impatient, task-focused manager may have to access some underdeveloped relationship skills if he is going to build an effective team. The detail-oriented technical expert may have to learn what it means to think strategically if she is going to have any hope of advancement in her organization.

As we have said, we seek form, structure, and meaning in life and then proceed to become limited by our forms, structures, and meanings. We develop our priorities and values—our truths—and then see them form limitations and boundaries around us. In much the same way, and as part of the very same dynamic, we find early in our lives a "formula for success." It is a set of behaviors, attitudes, and practices that seems to work for us. "We get recognized and rewarded for our efforts" says Robert Quinn in his book *Deep Change*. "Positive experiences validate our worldview, map script, myth, or paradigm. We know that we are all right—we have the historical evidence to prove it."

Then we build upon that formula, hand over hand, constructing our lives on the assumption that success will follow uninterrupted despite life's changing circumstances, if only we will stick to the formula.

This is a down-to-earth version of what the psychologists call complex formation, and it is a universal human phenomenon. In essence, it is a reflex in the present that has its genesis in the past. The psyche surveys a situation, or a problem to be solved, or a success needful to be had, and asks, *When have I been here before?* And even though the current situation may be only remotely similar, or the outer circumstances may have changed completely, the historically conditioned response is still triggered.

Though complex formation and "formulas for success" are universal phenomena, they are at the crux of one of life's most basic but neglected laws—and one that hit our postal service executives with the force of a revelation: *To continue your formula for success beyond its useful life is a recipe for failure, unhappiness, or even disaster.* In the context of business or organizational life, it means the things that made you successful in the first half of your career will not sustain you in the second and may even contribute to your undoing—unless you learn to change, adapt, grow, and mature as you navigate the second foundational shift.

The Center for Creative Leadership has studied the reasons for managerial "derailment" (getting involuntarily stalled, demoted, or fired) for the past three decades. While there are several principal reasons why managers fail, they each have one thing in common: there is an attempt to play life's second half by the same rules that governed the first—to enter new territory with an old and outdated map. Then, confronted with the baffling frustration of a formula that no longer works, the manager clings ever more tenaciously to past assumptions and behaviors, not realizing the "tried and true" has become "tired and false." When that happens, observes Quinn, "Our certainty that our old map must work drives us into a state of great pain and frustration. Only when our pain gets excruciating are we willing to humble ourselves and consider new actions that might allow us to successfully progress in our new situation."

At the end of the day in Potomac, Maryland, that's exactly where our four postal executives found themselves.

JAMES SIMONTON

James Simonton knows about the tried and true changing into its opposite at midlife. He refers to it as "the wall," and he found it in a small Asian sultanate a world away from his native England. As a promising young manager with an international financial institution,

James began his career as a self-described "fix-it guy" assigned to turn around underperforming constituent banks throughout the continent of Africa. He would hit the ground and could within a matter of weeks use his well-honed tactical acumen to determine which processes needed to change and what personnel needed to be replaced in order for profitability to improve. Then he'd disappear as quickly as he came.

But then came a major shift in his career—and a major opportunity. He was put in charge of the bank's operations in a small but affluent Asian sultanate. His multicultural staff of around three hundred was clearly not performing up to potential, and it was once again time for him to use his experience and acumen to "fix" that. But there was much more to this assignment. He would be expected to stay at this post for two to three years, to build an effective team for his successor, and to prove he was capable of a broad range of management skills in order to prepare himself for a similar role in a larger country.

Suddenly, the simple application of his prior formula for success was insufficient for the challenges he faced. "I realized," he said, "that this was going to be far more difficult than I'd ever imagined; that it would call from me skills I'd scarcely used before—that perhaps I didn't possess at all." Worse still, he was keenly aware that failure to "build and sustain" this bank as opposed to just "fixing" it would likely mean the end of career-advancement opportunities for him.

It did not begin well. His no-nonsense manner was often construed as insensitivity, and his occasional moodiness was seen as simple rudeness. What's more, his British figures of speech were often misunderstood by his Asian colleagues, who seemed disposed to assume the worst from such miscommunications.

But in the next three years of our work together, I watched as he struggled and grew and changed in his efforts to negotiate his "wall." He was not without setbacks in that work, but he was persistent, consistent, and admirably open to learning and change. Critical benchmarks along the way included the entry of the word "vulnerability" into James's vocabulary—the realization that a leader has to allow himself to be known and seen as fallible, readily admitting his human foibles and mistakes. He learned to seek out almost constant feedback from others, including his administrative assistant, who was encouraged to call him on his occasional lapses in sensitivity. Perhaps most challenging was the fact that James had to move against the grain of both his own personality and Asian cultural norms by declining to be seen as the "leader with all the answers," insisting instead that his people come to consensus on important issues on their own. All of these behaviors were, it is safe to say, the complete opposite of the ways in which he had successfully done business in Africa.

James's ability to break through his personal wall had striking consequences for his business. During the last year of his assignment in the sultanate, the bank was more than 50 percent ahead of its profitability targets before the third quarter was even over. But consistent with his own personal breakthrough, the numbers were now less important to him than the way they had been achieved.

To quote James: "When I came here, the team was producing modest results at best. It was hard to even call them a team. But there is something completely different now about the way they work together. They are achieving *fantastic* things. It's very satisfying to know that when I leave here, I'll leave a legacy of a great team achieving great results."

And for the man personally? At age forty-four he is on to his next assignment as head of the bank's operations in a much larger country and economy—but with a legacy of scaling his own personal wall. "I realized that throughout my career I had been playing a role. I had played it so long and so well, I'd come to assume that's who I was. I had this mental model that said, in effect, *Yes, I'm acting in this certain unpleasant way, but I'm getting things done, so it's acceptable.* It's no longer acceptable now and no longer necessary. I can be more myself and actually be more effective than I'd ever hoped. You can't believe how freeing that is."

———

Jung lamented there were no colleges for forty-year-olds "to prepare them for their upcoming life and its demands ... No, thoroughly unprepared we take the step into the afternoon of life; worse still, we take this step with the false assumption that our truths and ideals will serve us as hitherto."

Because our path is largely unmarked, it makes our choices and decisions just that much more difficult. I fear that for every James

Simonton who scales the midlife wall through courageous choice and change, there is another potential leader who balks and stalls (in fact, we will meet one in the chapter titled "Mistakes"). And the tragedy of that is not so much the failure to reach career goals and potential—though that is one very unfortunate result—but the overall failure to let go of who we *think* ourselves to be in order to grow and develop into who we are *capable of being*.

The most recent research on managerial derailment finds that while the principal causes of such career failures have remained constant over time, the inability to grow, change, or adapt has migrated to the top of the list. According to an article by Ellen Van Velsor and Jean Brittain Leslie in the *Academy of Management Executive* (1995 Vol. 9 No. 4), "in the view of senior managers, the ability to adapt and develop in the face of change or transition is more important now than ever before. It appears to be a factor in two-thirds of all derailments both in Europe and in the United States."

Success creates failure? In a sense, the second foundational shift turns all our traditional notions about life and career on their ear. Instead of an (hopefully) ascending straight line, we are seeing more the image of a parabola. But here's the trick: the descent is not a decline. Midlife can be, and often is, a difficult time of life; but it can also be a time of growth, development, expansiveness, and renewed authenticity. In fact, if we try to cling to our life as we knew it on the upslope, we find the continued ascension we seek to be elusive and illusory. We find instead a rigidity, a hardness setting in, as we try to fortify our self-construct against the danger of incursion. Instead of the continued expansiveness we seek, we encounter instead a progressive narrowing of life.

In this "dark wood" of midlife, where, as Dante put it, "the right road was wholly lost," we would do well to rely less on our conventional notions about life and our own formula for success than on what developmental psychology has to teach us. The poet and playwright T. S. Eliot, himself a veteran of a transformative midlife transition, said it this way in his *Four Quartets:*

"There is, it seems to us,
At best, only a limited value
In the knowledge derived from experience.

The knowledge imposes a pattern, and falsifies,
For the pattern is new in every moment
And every moment is a new and shocking
Valuation of all we have been."

The Third Shift:
Leaning into Life

My fiftieth year had come and gone,
I sat, a solitary man,
In a crowded London shop,
An open book, an empty cup
On the marble tabletop.
While on the shop and street I gazed,
My body of a sudden blazed!
And twenty minutes more or less
It seemed so great, my happiness,
That I was blessed—and could bless.
—William Butler Yeats

I have often thought that the best way to define a man's character
would be to seek out the particular mental or moral attitude in
which, when it came upon him, he felt himself most deeply and
intensely active and alive. At such moments there is a voice inside
which speaks and says, "This is the real me!"—William James

FOR THOSE WHO NAVIGATE "well enough" through the second
foundational shift, the middle years can be a time of flourishing at
work, at home, and within. The tremors of the midlife crisis are now
more distant rumblings as we enter a period of relative stability in
our lives. People who have successfully gone through the second shift

often report a surge of optimism, confidence, and verve that was lost or diminished while they were in the throes of midlife, as if life's energy itself was looking for a new gradient down which to flow and has now found a favored course.

Midlife can be an experience of disintegration to some—a kind of "coming apart at the seams." For them, this more stable period that follows can seem like a steady reintegration of the constituent parts of their lives around the changes and choices that have been made. We may have reevaluated, and to some extent redefined the values and priorities that drove our lives in earlier years, but those values and priorities have now morphed into a new coda for living that seems more of a personal "fit" for us.

So we may be married to the same man or woman, but the way we experience and describe that relationship may have changed appreciably. We may not be doing the same type of work—or if we are, our attitude toward it and what we expect out of it may have changed. Indeed, the lives of some of the most recognizable figures in the arts and sciences bear testament to the fact that the greatest—and at the same time most nuanced and wise—human works often come in the years after a difficult, even debilitating midlife transition.

But perhaps the greatest gift of the middle years is that, if the first and second shifts have gone "well enough," it is no longer necessary to live life reflexively. We have ambition but are not controlled by it. We can have our passions but are not their servant. We still have, of course, our instinctual drives, but we suffer less from their tyranny. We *have* all those things as before, but *they* do not *have us*, and that makes all the difference.

And so it follows that our formula for success—that complex of behaviors, attitudes, and practices that fueled our rocket to the top of the parabola—now gives way to more conscious choices, options and possibilities. To the extent that we live less reflexively and unconsciously, we are capable of living more creatively and authentically. That is the central equation of midlife development.

The great German poet Goethe, whose masterpiece *Faust* was itself an epic of midlife trial and redemption for both the author and central character, once said that "for a man to achieve all that is demanded of him, he must regard himself as greater than he is." I take that statement to mean that we should shoot beyond the bounds of our ability or risk undershooting our potential. We only find out how far we can go by risking a step too far.

The truth embodied in this thought should be something of a mantra for a man or woman in the middle years. The demands of life and the challenges we face in our "flourishing forties" (as author Gail Sheehy calls them) call for a little dose of hubris, a swig of self-confidence, to allow us to achieve all we must and all we *can*.

But remember Dr. Jung's warnings. When the achievements of the "morning" have been attained, we risk damage to our very souls by trying to take the yearnings, earnings, ambitions, and conquests of that time of life unfettered into the "afternoon." Developmentally, it may be considered the purpose of life's third foundational shift to help us learn for ourselves the particular "laws" of *our* life's afternoon, to reconcile us to them, and to help us live our mature adulthood with even deeper integrity, authenticity, commitment, and outright happiness.

THE TASKS OF THE THIRD SHIFT

The third foundational shift (analogous to Levinson's "age fifty transition") shares some characteristics with the first such shift ("into your own"). There usually is not a particular marker event that ushers in a transition from a state of prior stability. While the reevaluations and modifications that can take place during that time of life are extremely important for the development and even the ultimate direction of one's life, there usually aren't the markings of the kind of crisis so often seen in the second foundational shift.

But that statement is only true for people who have done their work and navigated "well enough" through the midlife transition. For those who have made inadequate or unsatisfactory changes in midlife (or have successfully ignored the process altogether), those chickens will most assuredly come home to roost in their fifties, as we will see a bit later in this chapter.

While there is generally no clear demarcation for the third shift, there are a host of events taking place during this time of life that help prepare the soil for the growth and transition to come. I call these events, collectively, "nature's conspiracy."

No matter how much we would like to envision our lives as continued upward expansiveness, we are unlikely to get away with that illusion for long. Slowly but inexorably we experience a decline in our physiological functioning. A long-time friend once observed, only half-jokingly, that during our twenties all he and I seemed to talk about was women; during our thirties, sports; but after that our conversations seemed to focus on our "procedures." By our fifties, practically none of us can hike as far, lift as much, or work without sleep for as long as we once could. Friends fall ill or even die, cracking the thin defenses of our thoughts of immortality. Parents or significant elders pass on, and we find ourselves attending as many funerals as we used to attend weddings. Children move on with their lives, and such weddings as we do attend, we often pay for!

As Professor Robert Kegan points out, our working lives are often in a similar state of flux in our fifties. On the one hand, we may feel our career is culminating, and we may be turning our attention to retirement, whatever that term may mean for us. It may feel more like "putting in time" to get to some career finish line. Or we may feel better postponing or ignoring thoughts of what that future might bring. In any event, we are generally in a mode of evaluating what we have done with our working lives and feeling a sense of satisfaction, disappointment, or an admixture of both.

Against this backdrop of inner and outer changes, the third transitional shift unfolds. My work with people in this time of life has taught me that there are three critical and interrelated tasks that are necessary to navigate this transition well and wisely.

First, we must come to reconcile—each for our own individual selves—the paradox between our *uniqueness* and our *ordinariness*. Most people emerge from midlife with some degree of imbalance between those two truths of our humanity, and it often takes the third shift for us to claim that pole within us, which has been most neglected. Our fifties are a most propitious time for encountering our limitations—and thus our commonality with the rest of humankind—and it is also a time for the exploration of possibilities that spring from our uniqueness and our gifts.

Second, we have to determine what we are going to leave in and what we will leave out. As you focus on the coming years and decades of your mature adulthood, the image of unpacking and repacking your bags should begin to resonate. You can't take all of it with you, and you shouldn't even try. It will only weigh you down. Who and what—people, purposes, places, and passions—do you want accompanying you forward?

And third, there is a need that beats within the breast of every human being to be remembered, to have made a difference, to leave a legacy. Some of life's most emotional losses—a special friendship, a long-term marriage, a defining job—are characterized by a feeling that we were just a "hole in the water," which seemed to close back up as soon as we were out of the picture. We can feel the third shift truly underway within us when we start to experience the human urge to leave a lasting imprint. It is then that we begin to complete the journey from adolescent illusions of immortality to a mature understanding that we can make lasting impressions on the world around us through our work, our families, our actions, and our love.

TED AND TOLSTOY

For any of the important life tasks of the third foundational shift to be accomplished, you must actually reach that point of transition in your life. And your chronological age is no guarantee you will. As we have noted, a transition delayed is not a transition successfully skipped, and there are many who, well into their sixth decade on Earth, have had an insufficient working through of the tasks of midlife. It will take years before they are ready for the third shift.

We have a good historical example in Leo Tolstoy, as writers will usually leave us a good paper trail of their own lives. It was only around the age of fifty that Tolstoy began to exhibit some of the more classic symptoms of a midlife crisis. In his own words:

> I felt that something had broken within me on which my life had always rested, and that I had nothing left to hold on to, and that morally my life had stopped ... It was an aspiration of my whole being to get out of life.

> All of this took place at a time when so far as my outer circumstances went, I ought to have been completely happy. I had a good wife who loved me and whom I loved; good children and a large property which was increasing with no

pains taken on my part. I was more respected by my kinsfolk and acquaintances than I had ever been; I was loaded with praise by strangers; and without exaggeration I could believe my name already famous. Moreover, I was neither insane nor ill … And yet, I could give no reasonable meaning to any actions of my life. And I was surprised that I had not understood this from the very beginning.

Tolstoy finally achieved a working through of a genuine midlife crisis with his novel *The Death of Ivan Ilyich*. It was the story of a wealthy lawyer consumed with his own career and unconcerned with the larger questions of life until stricken with a fatal illness. This powerful story—and cathartic work for its author—was published when Tolstoy was fifty-eight.

A little closer to home, and to the modern day, is my client Ted Bingham. To me, Ted is one of the really "good guys" of business. That is part of the reason his story is unpleasant to tell. In the years I knew and worked with him as a client, I never heard anyone speak ill of him as a person, even in the slightest. He was a good coach and mentor for his people, always preferring to teach rather than criticize. He was calm under pressure and reserved in his emotions. He was terrific at building consensus, but by his own admission was not a great negotiator. "That requires that you sometimes be intentionally unreasonable, and that's not my style," he'd say.

He had come by all of those positive characteristics quite naturally: an "Andy of Mayberry" kind of childhood in a small Southern town; full scholarship to a prestigious university in his chosen area of technical expertise; and thirty years of employment at the same Fortune 500 company at ever-increasing levels of responsibility. To boot, he had raised two daughters to productive adulthood and was still married to the vivacious woman who had been his childhood sweetheart and "soul mate."

At age fifty-five, Ted was a senior vice president of a diversified international company, with a seat on the executive committee and responsibility for several operating units. And as far as he was concerned, there was only one more rung on the ladder: promotion to executive vice president and a de facto role as elder sage of the executive committee. From there, clear sailing into retirement.

But that was not to be. The changes taking place around Ted were neither radical nor sudden, but even he says now in hindsight, "I really should have seen this coming." As international competition increased and margins for his company's products continued to shrink, the kinds of things that had earned him the respect and even affection of the people around him now started to flip into negatives. His preference for coaching over criticism now looked like being "too forgiving" of his managers and unable to "pull the trigger" on people quickly enough. His signature calm reserve now seemed to his peers to evidence a "lack of a sense of urgency and pressure around results," and they privately doubted whether he had "that edge or drive for profit." Ted prided himself on his ability to create compromise solutions, but that was now labeled "conflict avoidant." And while the company's genteel culture would never own up to this, there was a group of emerging leaders, five to ten years Ted's junior, who saw clearly the downsides of his style and were all too willing to exploit them.

At the same time the outer world was changing around him, Ted's inner landscape was shifting as well. Here's how he described it:

> At some point—and I'm not even sure when this started happening—I just began to lose some of the energy I had around certain things. This may sound silly, but the first time I noticed it was around sports. I'm a huge fan of [his alma mater's] football team, and I used to get so excited on the Friday before the first home game that I couldn't sleep that night. It was like Christmas for a little kid. I don't know how it happened but I just can't summon up that feeling anymore. What's worse, I can't get that feeling about *anything* anymore. There's just never that kind of delirious joy.

> I've been doing a lot of thinking about that and how it affects work. I'm successful and I enjoy what I'm doing, but I don't really have something to be passionate about. The biggest question in my mind right now is, what would bring me back that kind of passion?

Remember Charles Handy's axiom: "It is one of the paradoxes of success that the things and ways that got you there are seldom those things that keep you there." At the same time Ted was experiencing some of the classic symptoms of the midlife shift (loss of energy, lack of fulfillment), his outer world was changing around him in ways that thwarted his "formula for success" and actually turned it against him. He had hit "the wall," but unlike James Simonton, he was unable to grasp its meaning and significance and was thus unable to respond consciously to its challenges.

On top of that, Ted was now well into his fifties and was starting to feel the characteristic physiological changes that often take place during that decade. He became less physically active, adding more weight to his already sizable frame and moving a bit more slowly—none of which contributed positively to perceptions of Ted in a culture that valued the nimble and the quick.

The story, purely from a career perspective, does not end well. While Ted has kept his title and compensation, he has seen many of his businesses moved out from under his wing during the past two years. He knows the title of executive VP is out of reach. And if there is ever a change at the very top of the organization, one could imagine that Ted's job could be in jeopardy. Any one of those young Turks courteously waiting in the wings would love to have a shot at his position.

Why was Ted's midlife shift so out of season? How can life's flow come to be so ignored or postponed that we lose our chance to effectively navigate it?

Ted answered a similar question this way, beginning with a deep, rich laugh:

My wife, Betsy, says I was just too busy to fit in a midlife crisis. I was too busy for a lot of things, to tell the truth. The girls turned out great, but I feel like I missed a lot with them. I worked an inordinate number of hours and weekends. I missed some birthdays and anniversaries. Personal golf trips got cancelled; things like that. I loved what I did and I did what I loved; but if you ask me if I ever stepped back and looked at a bigger picture and made any decisions or changes around what I saw—no, I can't say that I made time for that.

And there's another part of this. I call it the "golden handcuffs." We grew up poor. I took away from that that the way to preserve your family's financial health was to put your hand to the plow, put your head down, and keep moving straight ahead. I didn't have a great desire to kick the traces, so to speak, but for financial reasons I couldn't afford to if I'd wanted. I guess I didn't feel like I had the freedom—and certainly didn't give myself permission—to think about approaching life any other way.

Regrets are only illuminations come too late. In that sense, Ted looks back upon his career without disappointment or remorse, but with the simple regret that he didn't examine his options—or indeed recognize that he had any. If at, say, age forty-five, he had loosened the golden handcuffs, put aside his "plow straight ahead" formula for success, and quit looking at the mule's butt in front of him for long enough to see the entire field, he might have made some different choices in time for them to have worked a difference in his life. Or he might have chosen not to do anything differently. But they would have been choices.

While the career story doesn't end well, Ted Bingham's personal story reads very differently. Here is how he describes his life and work at age fifty-seven:

I feel better about balance in my life than I've ever felt. I'm not as stressed out about things as I used to be. Betsy goaded me about buying a house at the beach until I relented, and we spend a lot of weekends there now with the girls and their families. My time away from work is more my time now. But interestingly I feel a whole lot more engaged at work too. I realize that I know more about certain aspects of our business than anybody else in the company—anybody anywhere, really—and I'm using that to our advantage. Even more important to me, I'm using the interest I've always had in coaching others to bring along folks who'll be running this company after I'm gone. That's really important to me.

Realizing his limitations while exercising his gifts; deciding what to leave in and what to leave out as the next phase of life unfolds; leaving an indelible legacy both at work and at home—Ted Bingham is hard about the tasks of the third foundational shift. And he is succeeding even better than "well enough."

Let's turn our attention to each of those tasks in turn.

ACCEPTING OUR LIMITS, CLAIMING OUR GIFTS

Uniqueness and ordinariness: our limitations and our giftedness—on which side of that human equation do you find yourself most often residing? As we have said, men and women who have successfully navigated the second shift often mount the challenges of their "flourishing forties" with an emphasis on their gifts and uniqueness. We flash them to the world, and in the mirror, in order to accomplish all of which we are capable. But if all goes well, we will not be out of balance for very long, for "nature's conspiracy" will serve to reacquaint us with our limitations and vulnerabilities.

If we are not so fortunate, we may find ourselves stuck on one side of the human equation or the other, with dramatically negative consequences for our continued growth and development. Consider my client Harriett. Her story might seem a bit extreme, but it is emblematic of those who enter the third foundational shift still ensnared (enslaved?) by their limitations.

You'd never know it to meet her. Harriett is one of the most classically attractive fifty-year-old women you will ever see. Fit and feminine, she is bright, well-educated, personable, and compassionate toward others. Yet to hear her talk about her life and work you would think she was living in a prison with very real if invisible bars. She spends her days in a windowless office doing repetitive and uninteresting work that does not challenge her in any positive way, yet it has been five years since she has floated a resume. "I just don't know what else I'm qualified to do," she says in resignation. She would like to move out of the small town where she was born, and with the children now out of the house, she has the financial independence to do so. But, "My parents need me," she says with a disturbing undercurrent of resentment. And despite the fact that it has been ten years since her divorce, she can count on one hand (with a couple of fingers to spare) the number of dates she has had. "I thought I'd be married again by now," she says sadly.

It is as if Harriett has had an extended lover's quarrel with life, which shows no signs of relenting. Nothing is good enough. Nobody is good enough. And of course the most dangerous heresy of all: *she* is not good enough—or smart, or talented, or deserving, or lucky enough. As author Kathleen Brehony points out, by the time many of us have reached midlife, we have lost that vital connection with our creative selves in favor of "being a member of the audience, sacrificing our uniqueness, our most creative voice, to the everyday realities of earning a living and taking care of our responsibilities. Most of the time we fail even to interject our own style and vision into our own daily lives."

This is the furthest thing from living with and embracing our limitations; it is becoming pathologically imprisoned by them. For those so incarcerated, one has to wonder what they fear most: failure or success? Do they cling to their ordinariness because they fear their uniqueness?

Those in such an illusory prison might do well to consider the words of Nelson Mandela, a man who lived in a very real prison for twenty-eight years:

> Our deepest fear is not that we are inadequate. Our deepest fear is that we are powerful beyond measure. It is our light, not our darkness, that most frightens us. We ask ourselves, who am I to be brilliant, gorgeous, talented, and fabulous? Actually, who are you *not* to be? You are a child of God. Your playing small doesn't serve the world. There is nothing enlightened about shrinking so that other people won't feel insecure around you. As we let our light shine, we unconsciously give other people permission to do the same.

The equal and opposite challenge of our maturity is that we not become in thrall of our uniqueness. "It is a supreme challenge," said Jung, "to ask man to become conscious of [both] his uniqueness and limitation. Uniqueness and limitation are synonymous. Without them, [there is] merely a delusory identity which takes the form of intoxication with large numbers and an avidity for political power."

Here's betting John Edwards would agree with that quote. In the summer of 2008, the handsome and charismatic politician was forced to admit he'd had, and then consistently lied about, an extramarital affair while running for president of the United States. Moreover, his wife of more than thirty years was being treated for terminal cancer at the time. While such peccadilloes are unfortunately all too common on the national stage, Edwards's explanation did evidence an honest understanding of the dynamic involved:

> I went from being a senator, a young senator to being considered for vice president, running for president, being a vice presidential candidate, and becoming a national public figure. All of which fed a self-focus, an egotism, a narcissism that leads you to believe that you can do whatever you want. You're invincible. And there will be no consequences.

John Edwards's story and his resulting ignominious exit from public life is but one vignette showing what can happen when there is an overload on the other side of the uniqueness/limitation equation. It can happen whenever our gifts are deemed to be our personal possessions, tools to be used for our own aggrandizement. Neither this nor the imprisonment of our limitations should be our fate.

Just to be clear: you don't need to be a nationally known politician to be an idiot. In Key West, from whence I write this, I can watch the fifty-something men and their decades-younger girlfriends playing a sort of game that requires blindness to one's limitations and the enthronement of one's uniqueness (or the illusion thereof). "Come on, Sugar Pants, let's get back to the hotel," the man calls out in exasperation to his paramour as she ducks inside yet another overpriced jewelry store, the terms of the day's barter still unsettled. Now, I believe as much as anyone in the possibility of May/September romances, but—trust me on this—that wasn't what was happening here. Praise the Lord and pass the Viagra.

So what does the balance look like when finely struck? I'm betting you have as many examples around you as I do. It's all in knowing what to look for. It might resemble my sister, Bethany, now fifty-five, who has suffered the ravages of juvenile-onset diabetes to the point of disability yet has eschewed the victim role in favor of her important work as director of volunteer services for a major medical center. Or there's my wife of thirty-nine years, who transmuted an inability to have biological children into raising two wonderful adopted daughters and a career as one of our state's leading legal experts on child protection. It is as if limitation worked together with giftedness, each to make the most of the other.

Or there's my long-time friend Steve McKaig. When he graduated from college, Steve bought a small interest in an insurance agency. Hard work and the retirement of his older partners put him in a position to purchase the agency outright in his early forties. Genial and unassuming, yet smart and industrious, Steve steadily grew the business in his thriving hometown market, eventually opening two satellite offices in nearby towns.

At age fifty-six he got an exciting opportunity to merge with another firm. For Steve that would mean that, if nothing went unexpectedly wrong, he would have the chance to nearly double his income potential and assure a most favorable retirement. But there were two major downsides. He would have to take on a sizable amount of debt in order to make the deal happen. Equally important was the knowledge that he would be committing himself to work much harder, for longer hours, for many more years, before his investment would fully pay off.

Steve got all the way to the literal deadline for closing the transaction before deciding what to do. Here's how he describes his dilemma and its resolution:

> There's no doubt this would have been the ideal opportunity for me ten years ago. But I really felt a conflict. I'm a grandfather now, and I can tell you that gives you an entirely new perspective on how you want to spend your time. Plus, I really like to travel, and I don't think I can fool myself into thinking I can do that forever. I love history and want to write like you do. My world is really expanding, and I don't want to narrow my focus merely to work and paying off loans. In the past fifteen years I've had skin cancer and major back surgery, and I've come around to thinking that life is both fragile and dynamic. It's precious both because it's terminable and because it's so full of possibilities. How much of that do I want to invest in making money as opposed to enjoying time and the people around me to the max? So I passed.

We said earlier that one of the hallmarks of midlife maturity is the ability to see the truth in contradiction and paradox. The opposite of something that is dear and true to us can itself contain some degree of truth, while our most deeply held beliefs are subject to some degree of error. So it is with the paradox of uniqueness and limitation. If we can accept the fact that there are boundaries to life, just as there are to the life of the organism itself, then we can cease our clamoring to expand life "beyond the bounds of all reason and sense," as Jung warned. We can, for example, accept that making it to the round of eight at the great Wimbledon of corporate succession has actually made for a pretty satisfying career. We can, along with Charles Handy, chuck our endless "image enhancement" in favor of the realization that "the nice thing about growing older is that you eventually stop pretending ... and discover that being oneself, being truly oneself, is really rather fun." We can take care of the health of our bodies without fooling ourselves about them or wishing they were other than they are. And we can let "Sugar Pants" go buy her own damned jewelry.

On the other side of the coin, we can just as equally and even more eagerly embrace and claim our unique gifts. No more hiding them in the name of conformity; no more being embarrassed by them; no more "playing small."

One of the reasons this particular task of the third shift is so important is because it is as eminently practical as it is necessary. When that balance is finely drawn, it opens up a world of realistic possibilities for your life and work that you may never have conceived before. In fact, *possibility* now becomes the operative word, supplanting both the defeatism that comes from an overfocus on our limitations and our unrealistic expectations of the world that spring from our narcissistic "specialness." We are free to be real. And like Steve McKaig, we are free to make choices that balance our personal limits with an equally personal, compelling future.

Those who pass through the third shift find that one of its most delectable fruits is a realization that they are possessed of what they need to be reasonably happy in their life and work as they enter their mature years. They don't see their limitations and shortcomings as barriers but rather as aspects of themselves to be acknowledged, sidled up to, befriended. It is not resignation or passive acceptance but a leaning fully into life with all its challenges and blessings.

At the same time, they recognize their talents and are often exploring new ones, appropriating them as the boons they are. But their reach no longer exceeds their grasp. What they need, they have.

It is in the work of Wendell Berry that I find the best expression of this thought—the fruit of the balance finely struck. From his poem "The Wild Geese":

Horseback on Sunday morning,
harvest over, we taste persimmon
and wild grape, sharp sweet
of summer's end. In time's maze
over the fall fields, we name names
that went west from here, names
that rest on graves. We open
a persimmon seed to find the tree
that stands in promise,
pale, in the seed's marrow.
Geese appear high over us,
pass, and the sky closes. Abandon,
as in love or sleep, holds
them to their way, clear,
in the ancient faith: what we need
is here. And we pray, not
for a new earth or heaven but to be
quiet in heart, and in eye
clear. What we need is here.

LEAVING IN AND LEAVING OUT

Norton Tennille is something of an expert in the art of unpacking and repacking bags. What's more, no one would ever accuse him of being timid about what to leave in and what to leave out.

At age fifty-three, the former Rhodes Scholar and Harvard Law grad had established himself as one of the better-known environmental lawyers in Washington, DC. A chance meeting with a young South African lawyer led Tennille to visit the Horn of Africa in 1994. While watching the Atlantic and Indian oceans collide just outside Cape Town, a thought descended on him: "This is the place for me."

"It was pretty close to an epiphany", says Tennille, "but in fairness I had been thinking about getting out of DC for so long." With that, he traveled back to Washington, closed down his law practice of more than twenty years, and began a new life and career in his adopted country. Now his South African Education and Environmental Project helps schoolchildren at all levels and in many ways, from training in computer technology to poetry and debate workshops.

South Africa was a turbulent place in 1994, emerging from decades of apartheid to a democratically elected and inclusive government. "There were predictions of bloodbaths," Tennille said. "A lot of people questioned my sanity."

The decisions necessary to leave behind the safety and comforts of the United States, his extended family, and (gulp) a lucrative law practice were difficult, yet the path ahead seemed clear—especially when it came to his work. "Even though it was an exciting career, I was doing most of my work for corporations, and I found very little socially redeeming value in it."

Now, says one of his South African board members, "He has a sincerity of mission and purpose. There is nothing whatsoever in it for him. It's all about making a difference in the lives of children in Cape Town."

And what advice would Norton Tennille have for those of us who are understandably more timid in our choices? "This is a classic case of letting yourself fall and letting the world support you. You never know what is going to happen when you let go."

Most of us are not called to be Norton Tennilles and go halfway around the world to do something more "socially redeeming." But he would never have made it past the DC city limits if he had not made some hard and conscious choices about what he wanted to leave in and leave out in this next phase of his life. The accumulated weight would otherwise simply have been too great.

And so, an important task of the third foundational shift is to shed those things that impede us, retain and feed those things that enliven us, and have the wisdom to know the difference.

Men and women in their fifties will often begin a period of consolidation, beginning with places and things. We may sell that place at the lake whose upkeep is no longer worth the time we spend there. We may downsize our living quarters to something more manageable—after all, the kids have their own places now, and they could sure use some of this furniture. We may build a cabin on that lot in the mountains, and then watch as we fill it with so many of our most loved belongings that it starts to feel like the "real" home to us. We rent storage units, clean out attics, and give stuff away until the "essentials" remain.

As much as we may hate to admit it, much of the same consolidation begins to happen with the people in our lives. As the natural attrition in our circle of friends takes place through moves, job changes, and even death, we find we don't usually replace them with new, close friends. We still host and go to parties and have our community activities, but the circle of people we feel we can call with a serious problem at four in the morning dwindles to a precious few.

At the same time (as the phenomenon of Classmates.com and similar sites show us), there is a desire to reach out and touch those who were close to us in our formative years, as if our shared history created something of a shared essence. And it's all about the "essentials" at this time of life, which is why the superficial and superfluous—the people we knew only because we were fellow soccer moms and dads or part of the same office staff—gradually fade from view.

This is healthy. We may look around wistfully from time to time and wonder where all those folks went, but the simple truth is, what you need at this time of life are those who feed your heart and soul most deeply, who know you most essentially, and who give you comfort and support (either overtly or wordlessly) in your continued growth and development. They should be with you as you unpack and repack your bags because they will help you carry them forward.

What you distinctly do *not* need are those people who will weigh you down or get in your way. They most commonly come in the form of friends or extended family with whom you once shared common experiences or interests but who expect you to be and act the same way now that you did then. They need that for themselves, as some sort of reassurance that things and people don't change. But they *do* change, and to give them what they need can be—at least beyond a certain point—a trap for you.

Finally, like Norton Tennille, you may come to find that your job, or occupation, or even your chosen career is something you must "leave out" as you focus on your remaining working years. At the least, you may discover that you can only leave it "in" if you make some significant changes.

This too is enormously healthy. Far too many men and women in the third foundational shift are weighed down by their own stubborn self-definitions, which equate their personal merit with their job title. Their anxiety is reflected in the questions they will ask of me when we discuss their career options: "If I just up and make a change, what will people think of me?" "Don't people usually assume you were fired when you change jobs?" "Won't people assume I just don't know what I want to do when I grow up?"

The anxiety is understandable and a part of the process, but you will notice that each objection has to do with what other people might think. That is why it is such a critical part of post-midlife maturity that we have a more inner-based system of worth and merit. That too is part of what leaning into life—this third shift—is all about.

Besides that, it has been my experience that the fears my clients have about others' perceptions are exaggerated. I agree with Gail Sheehy that "there is generally no accepted point in the career cycle when men are expected to say: *I've done my duty, I've proven myself, I'm not going to do the same thing anymore* ... Today, there is plenty of time for a man to reinvent himself for a Second Adulthood." And when they do, others admire them more than question them and wonder why they didn't have the courage to do the same thing.

The more fundamental aspects of making life choices that involve relationships and career are treated more deeply in the next two chapters. For now, suffice it to say they are generally the two most critical arenas for deciding what to leave in and what to leave out.

THE PASSIONATE LIFE

By deciding what to leave out, you make room for what you wish to carry with you. Yes, in our fifties there are still commitments, obligations, and responsibilities. But there is room too for those things that tap into our *passion*, and it is those things that lend excitement, joy, texture, and vibrancy to our mature years.

Joseph Campbell made famous the advice to "follow your bliss," but I think the word "passion" is closer to our meaning here. It connotes such a strong affection, enthusiasm, and zeal for something that we absolutely *must* carry it with us, as our life would seem dry and tasteless without it. It would cause us too much suffering (one original meaning of the word "passion") if we somehow couldn't take it along.

Passion is that life force Thomas Wolfe referred to when he said, "I want to loot my life clean" while he still could. It accounts for why William Butler Yeats was still writing poetry on his deathbed. It is why Degas spent the last twenty years of his life in a solitary brown studio, painting only for himself but determined to create something of great beauty. And it's why my friend Sam Matthews, once head of information services for massive Wachovia Bank, now directs a small nonprofit that provides programs for seniors. "I'm really not into retirement," he says. "I get jazzed over getting things done."

In fact, Sam is but one example of a rapidly growing phenomenon known as "encore careers." A recent survey found that of the seventy-eight million American baby boomers now hitting retirement age, more than half were interested in starting a new career with a positive social impact. So Robert Weisberg, after a life in the US foreign service and a stint as ambassador to the Congo, now heads the international ethics office for Nokia. Joseph Kilpatrick, former associate director of the Z. Smith Reynolds charitable foundation, offers free consulting services to smaller nonprofits. Peter Agre won the 2003 Nobel Prize for chemistry and had a cushy job at Duke University, but he took a pay cut in order to head the Malaria Research Institute at Johns Hopkins. All made the move while in their fifties and arguably at the height of their professional power, but each was even more passionate about the road ahead. Said Agre, "It wasn't a matter of being a Mother Teresa. It was a matter of, 'Boy, that sounds like fun.'"

What each of those disparate people and personalities has in common is that they each made a decision to lead a passionate life. Understanding their limitations and their gifts, they chose to claim and live out of their giftedness, whatever form it might take. And they made choices about what to leave out and what to leave in, in order to make room for what seemed most essential.

During the first few decades of our lives, there are large chunks of our life and work that remain "provisional": "I will stay with this job, provided …"; "I will stay in this marriage, provided …"; "I will live in this city/community/neighborhood, provided …" We keep our options open, our plan B intact, and in many instances that is both healthy and necessary.

But "provisional" is the opposite of "committed," and the ability to commit to a certain path or place or person increasingly becomes a mark of maturity as we move into our fifties. Degas and Yeats were committed to their craft; Norton Tennille and Sam Matthews to the service of something beyond themselves; my parents (and perhaps yours) to each other. There was no, "Well, if this doesn't work out, then ..." Through deprivations, hardships, or disappointments, each remained committed to the object of their passion.

Of course, commitment and passion do not belong solely to the third foundational shift. But the cycle of life does seem to deliver us to a place, often in our fifties, where the provisional life starts ever more fully to give way to the committed life—where, by deciding what we will leave in and what we will leave out going forward, we discover (or rediscover) those things we are most passionate about, and we invest ourselves more fully in them.

"In the final analysis," says Jung, "we count for something only because of the essential we embody, and if we do not embody that, life is wasted."

EARLY DREAMS, MATURE LEGACIES

The desire to leave something behind that outlasts our own lives is an ancient and primal urge. We share that instinctual drive with many other creatures. But rather than focusing exclusively on the propagation of young and the preservation of herd or hive, humans are able to conceptualize the possibility of leaving their mark in an infinite variety of ways. But whatever the means, psychologists, sociologists, and anthropologists agree there is a fundamental human urge to produce that which will outlast us, something that impels us to sow what we will never reap.

The legacy we wish to leave does not spring forth fully formed, like Athena from the head of Zeus, once we begin the third foundational shift. It is instead part of developmental process that has its origins very early in life.

Think back to your earliest fantasies about what you "wanted to be when you grew up." Movie star? Carnegie Hall impresario? Pro Bowl quarterback? Howard Hughes? Or perhaps your secret fantasy was a bit more modest—a teacher, firefighter, or revered parent. Think also about the things you most enjoyed doing, those moments when you felt most alive, those stretches where you were oblivious to the passage of time because you were so in thrall of what you were doing.

These were not meaningless childhood fantasies. They were, instead, the acorn of your individuality taking root in you. They were the first evidence of what many writers have called "The Dream"—our earliest vision as children of the kind of lives we wished to lead as adults and the kinds of activities that would generate for us the greatest excitement and vitality. Because The Dream does not generally come true in a literal way, we adults may patronize or deride it ("Isn't that cute?") but fail to see that The Dream thinly masks qualities and traits to which the child will aspire as an adult—artistic talent, competitiveness, nurturance, or downright heroism, as examples. And, to our surprise, men and women who navigate "well enough" the three foundational shifts may find their early dream has much to say about their later legacy.

Some version of The Dream, even if poorly articulated and only tenuously connected to reality, will typically appear in a child between the ages of three and eight and then reemerge with renewed force during adolescence. The timing is not accidental. These are the points in younger life when purely genetic influences hold the least sway, and the child is freer to develop his or her own personal myth for how adulthood should be lived out.

We rarely achieve the expansive dreams of our youth in just the form or fashion they were first imagined. And that is undoubtedly a good thing. George Bernard Shaw observed that there are two tragedies in life: one is not to get your heart's desire and the other is to get it. But the truth is, life will almost never allow us to achieve the omnipotent dreams of childhood, and those few who do (think of child actors and rock stars, among others) often find their success comes at great peril to both body and soul.

What happens instead for most of us is that The Dream gets "realized." We don't have the talent or the time to be that star athlete or dancer, or the income potential to be Donald Trump, or the depth to be the next Carl Sandburg. Maybe we just wanted to be super-mom or super–dad, and the kids had the temerity not to turn out very well. The Dream collides with life-as-it-is.

But it is actually one of the finer accomplishments of the *first* foundational shift—occurring in our twenties and thirties—if we can take the passion and exuberance that infused the dreams of our youth and give it a more mature form and structure in our adulthood. Remember that, as we discussed earlier, a central task of the first foundational shift is to free ourselves of the expectations of others *and from our own*. Thus, as Levinson observed, "When a man no longer feels that he must be a remarkable writer, craftsman, or leader, he is more free to be himself and to work according to his own wishes and talents."

While our youthful dream should not follow us unfettered into young adulthood, it would be an equal and opposite mistake to dismiss it altogether as childish nonsense. The Dream had a passion and a power behind it that was peculiar to you as an individual. It did not disappear, even though it may have changed its shape considerably or been neglected entirely in the service of the difficult tasks of adulthood.

I love immensely the story of Albert Einstein's Dream and how it reemerged for him in his twenties. As a young child, he was fascinated by the thought of riding on a beam of light speeding through the heavens. How thrilling that must have felt—how grand it must have seemed—to that odd-looking German Jewish boy with a significant speech impediment! Many years later, after toiling away yet another day as an anonymous clerk in a Swiss patent office, he was enjoying his favorite "childish" fantasy while riding on a bus speeding away from the Zurich clock tower. Suddenly his reverie turned to realization: if he were indeed riding on that beam of light instead of a rickety bus, the time shown on the clock would never seem to change—its light could never catch up to him! The passage of time is not an absolute but is relative to the velocity of light! At that moment, and out of that boyish fantasy, Einstein's theory of relativity was born.

As you approach the third foundational shift of life, The Dream will almost inevitably resurface. Once again, the timing is not surprising if you consider that in later adulthood, as in early childhood and adolescence, the human intelligence is less subject to purely hereditary influences. And The Dream will be visible to the naked eye in the kind of legacy you work to leave.

I'll begin with a personal example. When a young Michael Thompson was asked in grade school what he wanted to do when he grew up, this was his exact response: "I want to help people do what they can't do for themselves." What he had in mind when he said that was the image of Perry Mason, whom he watched at every opportunity on the little black and white TV in the living room. He dreamed of courtroom victories and public accolades and perhaps political office.

None of those things ever happened. The practice of law proved too unrelentingly contentious for my tastes, and I shifted my career more than once to find the right fit. But if you ask me today what I most enjoy and want to be remembered for in my work, my answer would be something like: "At least on my better days, I am able to help people accomplish in their lives and work things they might not have accomplished without a little help."

And, in case you're wondering, I wouldn't be laboring over this book if it didn't tap the energy and passion of my original Dream, or if I weren't so impelled to leave it behind for whatever use it may be to others.

The reason legacy comes to the fore as a task of the third foundational shift is because it becomes clear at this time of life that time is not unlimited. Death is no longer an abstraction in our fifties, something that happens to the old or unlucky, or to grandparents. It is happening to our own parents, friends, and colleagues—and it becomes frighteningly clear that it will ultimately happen to us.

As we make this transition, the growing recognition of our own mortality collides with the very human wish for immortality, which Levinson called "the strongest and least malleable of human motives." If we are going to come to terms with death as a reality and not an abstraction, something within us says, "Well, then, at least my life is going to have meaning and purpose and value. I'm not going to be a hole in the water when I leave this family, this work, or this life. Something is going to survive and be remembered. I will leave a mark, however small." Such is the motivation that powers the leaving of a legacy.

But what form that legacy will take, its individual shape and texture, is the product of one's individual dream. As part of the dynamic of the third foundational shift, we will start to recollect and reflect on that dream as part of an overall evaluation of what has been accomplished in our life. It is like a lighthouse beacon that has always been there, but we've been too busy sailing the high seas to pay it much mind. Now as we begin a turn toward our port of call, we recall it and are reminded of our need for it.

Unfortunately for some—and this is a great tragedy when it occurs—that beacon got extinguished somewhere along the way. Beaten down by circumstance or ill fortune, they have lost any connection they may have had to an enlivening personal dream (or, worse yet, never had one), and simply wither away or live out rather trivial lives in some small, accommodating corner of humanity. The plays of Henrik Ibsen, Eugene O'Neill, and Arthur Miller are full of such characters.

For the rest of us, the recollection of The Dream presents us with a singular opportunity to form a lasting legacy. Consider this reflection from writer James Baldwin:

> When more time stretches behind than stretches before one, some assessments, however reluctantly and incompletely, begin to be made. Between what one wishes to become and what one has become there is a momentous gap, which will now never be closed. And this gap seems to operate as one's final margin, one's last opportunity, for creation.

Seen in this way, The Dream is neither useless youthful fantasy nor an occasion for the mourning of lost innocence but a reclamation project for that which made you unique (there's that word again!) in the first place, and an opportunity for the creation of something lasting.

Allow a former client of mine, Norman Chung, to tell you how that works. "When I was a boy growing up in Singapore, I knew that I wanted to work in public service. Of course, being an ambitious young boy, I wanted it to be a very high position"—he laughs—"certainly minister of an important agency. These were the early boom times for the Singaporean economy, and I wanted to be in the middle of it."

For almost all his working life, Norman did in fact work in economic development for the government, holding a variety of management positions. But after he turned fifty, things began to change. While Singapore has a civil service code similar to that of the United States, it does not have age discrimination laws, and Norman found himself in a classic over-fifty edge-out. "They wouldn't fire me, but I felt an increasing lack of support. They wanted younger people, who might have less experience, but they could pay them less money."

It was now clear that the role he was in—deputy director—would be his terminal position. As a highly educated engineer, he could find work elsewhere and save his ego the daily beating it was absorbing. But he had not lost his enthusiasm for his job or for the difference he was making. "No, this is not what I once imagined for my career," he laments. "I will never become director of the agency despite my qualifications and experience, and that is not fair. But there is still much I can do.

"What is that word you Americans use? It may sound 'corny,' but I can make a contribution in the years I have left before I retire. I want to be remembered for my integrity, service, and hard work, and when they look at that work they will know that I accomplished something for the people of my country. I took a bad situation for myself and turned it into something good for others. That's something."

It is, indeed. It is the creation of a Legacy.

OF CHARACTER AND CALLING

In his book *The Soul's Code*, groundbreaking psychologist James Hillman puts forth and supports a fascinating thesis about human development. The ideas are not totally new; they go back at least as far as Plato. But in an age that permits of only two answers to the question of why we are as we are—heredity and/or environment—Hillman's voice for a third choice may seem rather radical. He proposes what he calls the "acorn theory," which holds that there is implanted within each of us a unique and innate image that gives us our sense of calling in life, forms our most essential character, and gives us the particularity we feel about ourselves.

While such a theory can neither be proven nor disproved, I find it compelling. It helps us understand the existence of The Dream as one of the early manifestations of the acorn. It would account for the "peek-a-boo" quality of The Dream as it shows its face in the particularities and peculiarities of our character, as it sometimes disappears altogether, and as it almost universally reappears as part of the third foundational shift. It would also help explain why pioneering developmental psychologist

Charlotte Malachowski Buhler, writing in the 1930s, thought she discovered a certain inner coherence or hidden "intentionality" in the lives of her patients, who were in their fifties.

And, most importantly, it makes room for the existence of a God who implants the acorn in the first place. When John Keats said, "I know nothing but the holiness of the Heart's affections and the Truth of the Imagination," I have always understood him to mean that the passions that make us unique are our brush with holiness, and that there was something eternally true about our childhood imaginings. The Dream is our link to the Ineffable.

Hillman's work also invites us to look at our traditional notions of "character" in a different light. A homogeneous society would like to think character consists in being the most homogenized one can be. It's safer that way. But character has very little to do with conformance to the conventional. It is instead, says Hillman, through "the oddities of character specific to our solitary uniqueness" that we become most truly ourselves and contribute most lastingly to the world around us. Rather than being immovably centered, then, the character that is truest to itself becomes capable of being eccentric—meaning, literally, off center—in the pursuit of our unique lives and calling.

It is that eccentricity of character that will itself form part of our legacy—the salty stories from that stint overseas, the quirky habits that used to drive others crazy, the unpopular stands taken or words spoken, even the self-righteous gossip of our detractors all contribute to the volume of work that will be stored in the memories of others. We make a difference because of our character and not our conformity, and it is that for which we will be remembered.

And how do we spot our own character when we see it playing itself out? Remember the quote from William James that opens this chapter. While we may find it hard to define character, it shows itself in the lives of each individual in those moments where they feel "most deeply and intensely active and alive." Passion portrays character and gives it face and form. It is when we feel most alive that it is most visible, to ourselves and to others. And when, in our maturity, we have negotiated the tasks of the third foundational shift, our true character will be closest to the surface of our lives and most easily claimed as our own.

Choices I:
Work, Jobs, and Career

You can't make someone else's choices. You shouldn't let someone else make yours.—Colin Powell

The hardest thing to learn in life is which bridge to cross and which to burn.—David Russell

OUR DAY-TO-DAY EXISTENCE IS full to the brim with choices. Get up with the alarm or hit the snooze bar? Brown or black shoes? Paper or plastic? But life saves its most important and often wrenching choices for the periods of foundational shift. The process and products of our choices are, in fact, at the very heart of any transitional shift in our lives. It must be so, because as Levinson observed, "In a transitional period one must terminate the existing structure, explore possibilities (in self and world) out of which new choices can be formed, and make the initial choices that provide the basis for a new structure."

Those choices will look different depending on the foundational shift one is facing. For a man in his twenties or thirties, the choices may be around building a life more consonant with personal driving values. In a woman's thirties or forties, the choices may be bound up in the predictable crises of the middle passage. One in his or her fifties may be hard about the task of deciding what to leave out and what to take along as he or she moves into mature adulthood. But for each, the developmental task is to provide, through "good enough" choices, a solid platform from which to proceed into the next phase of life. If he or she chooses poorly, or opts for no choice at all, an inner contradiction is set up that will only return later with greater seismic force.

The choices we are talking about here are important, often difficult, and do not yield to our traditional (at least Western) notions of how good decisions are made. You know the model very well: you simply list the "pros" on one side of a page and the "cons" on the other and get on with the business of making a logical choice. But anyone who has ever tried to use this simple T-chart for one of life's more troubling choices—whether to stay in a relationship or marriage; whether to stay in a particular job; whether we've chosen the right career—knows how fruitless such a solely left brain approach can be. We feel sundered by the decision, as evidenced by the way we describe it: "torn," "split," "divided." And while logic and experience should never be lost in the swirl of confusion that often surrounds such choices, they are also not the only tools we have at our disposal. We just have to know where else to look.

In the midst of my own third foundational shift, I had a dream that summed this up for me nicely. (I do pay attention to my dreams, in the ways and for the reasons set forth later.) When this particular dream came to visit, I was beset with questions about the path my work would take during the next few years of my life. I was quite appropriately doing my research, making my lists of pros and cons, and talking to trusted friends and mentors; but I had it in my mind that I *had* to come to a conclusion during a certain time frame.

During this time, coincidentally, the Beijing summer Olympics were proceeding, and like most Americans, I would check the medal count occasionally and watch an event of interest to me. In the dream, a new Olympic sport was being played for the first time this year. The event was called "waiting." A friend from childhood tells me in the dream that he has become involved in the sport quite by accident but now has become rather good at it and is in contention for a medal in Beijing. He explains to me the finer points of how one can continue to be patient even when the world is saying you have waited long enough.

Upon awakening, two things seemed clear. I think my dream had chosen my friend as a positive example because, in my waking life, I had much admired his maturity, thoughtfulness, and patience while dealing with a painful domestic situation. But the dream also gave me a strong message that while I was doing all of the appropriate, outwardly rational tasks necessary to make this important choice, I *also* needed to "work on my game" when it came to the equally important non-rational, non-Western art of waiting.

But waiting for what? It would be so much easier if we were able to ferret out the data needed for life's big decisions, load it into a computer somewhere, and have the "right" answer emerge. We could then silence those inner and outer voices that say, "Get on with it; what are you waiting for?"

But remember Jung's admonition that the most fundamental problems in life are not solved but outgrown. It is a *process, which goes on within the foundational shifts themselves*, which yields up the answers in time. As envisioned by Jung, this process begins with an internal clash of what feels like irreconcilable opposites: to stay in this marriage or to leave; to plug away at this job or not; to take this offer or that one. But what Jung noticed about his patients who worked through the process was the gradual emergence of an alternative that might bear little resemblance to either of the original opposites—a *third,* which became possible only because the patient gave the process time and space to work.

If we neither prematurely quit our job nor decide we're trapped, we may find a way to stay with greater freedom and satisfaction. If we neither run to an affair nor accept a dead marriage out of duty, we have a chance to feel revitalized in our relationship, or at least find a pathway out that is less destructive of the lives around us. If we do not feel a compulsion to choose between path A or path B within some arbitrary time frame, we may find a path C revealing itself to us in time. We can medal in the sport of "waiting."

As Jung put it, "Out of the collision of opposites the unconscious psyche always creates a third thing of an irrational nature, which the conscious mind neither expects nor understands. It presents itself in a form that is neither a straight 'yes' nor a straight 'no'". Jung called that process "the transcendent function," and we will visit it in more detail in the chapter "Safe Home." For those in the grip of one of life's most wrenching choices, it can be a saving grace.

THE PSYCHOLOGY OF OUR JOB CHOICES

Sigmund Freud was once asked how he could tell a psychologically healthy person. His response was brief and profound: *"Lieben und arbeiten"*—love and work. And while the choices and challenges that face us during life's foundational shifts are wide and varied, it is undeniably true that the thorniest among them—and therefore the most growth producing—have to do with our vocation and our relationships.

In some ways, the choreography of human growth and development seems to work at odds with a life of healthy work and vocation. We prepare and educate ourselves for a certain career, only to find that adjustments are necessary if we are to come "into our own" as individuals. Then, no sooner have we settled into productive professional lives than we find that our original "formulas for success" are starting to fail us, sending us into the serious reevaluations of midlife. Then that storm passes and we nestle into middle adulthood, only to be faced a few years later with the challenges and tasks of our fifties. At any of those shift points of life and work, with an infinite variety of intensities and symptoms, questions of career can emerge. It's simply a part of the process.

We witness the symptomatology, whether within ourselves or others. Outwardly we may seem moody or uncommunicative, or we may be whiney, complaining, and fault-finding about our situation and our coworkers (particularly bosses). But the inner dynamic is far more dramatic. We may have spent ten, twenty, maybe even thirty years building a career that doesn't now meet some of our most important needs. The flaws in what we have built may have existed for some time, but they are only now becoming intolerable. Time seems short and the stakes seem very high. And yet during those past years we have made commitments and built expectations, and it is very difficult to see how changes can be made without doing harm to others. To stay where we are feels like a kind of death; to go in another direction risks not only failure, but fail*ing* others. We are truly, like Odysseus of old, caught between Scylla and Charybdis.

For most people, a vocational choice that feels this wrenching will happen only once or twice in their working lives. Some of us have the distinction—if one can call it that—of having several such shift points during our careers. But there are two certainties. First, if the choice is poorly made or successfully ignored, it will resurface again in the next phase of life. In fact, your inner self may not allow you to wait that long. As psychiatrist Robert Gould points out, "When we're paralyzed by a vocational decision, our unconscious usually 'attempts a rescue' by forcing us to do something, [usually] by the breakthrough of some negative and potentially disastrous behavior or symptom" such as hypochondria, overuse of drugs or alcohol, self-destructive affairs, or poor judgment on crucial matters so as to engineer a failure.

Which leads us to the second truth: if you are conscious of what is going on and approach the vocational dilemma with all the faculties at your disposal, you have an infinitely better chance of choosing "well enough."

The first thing of which to be conscious is that you do not merely have a job title, you have a *role*. All human groups develop roles, which the members of the group are offered or even expected to play. The larger and more complex the group, the more tightly circumscribed the role. In that most highly complex of human groups—the modern corporation—the roles become exceptionally well-defined over time. We don't give them names, as we do our job titles, but you would be able to recognize them in any office environment, just as you could in the cast of any TV sitcom with a business setting: Mr. Charisma, the nurturing mother hen, the joker, the femme fatale, the nerd, the ditz, the scapegoat, and many more.

As Murray Stein has observed, what we call "corporate culture" is really a composite of these roles and how they are acted out; yet the individuals who comprise the corporation and occupy the roles are largely unconscious of how all of this works. We are rather like fish swimming in water when we are part of an organization's culture: we don't know that it's water and are quite oblivious to its makeup unless we are suddenly taken out of it.

The problem is that, as marvelously complex human beings, the organizational role can at best do justice to only a fragment of who we are. "All of us in organizations are 'role occupants,'" says Charles Handy, "and few of us could claim that there is a perfect match between us and our role. That, I think, is part of the problem with organizations and part of their seduction. They force us, or allow us, depending on your viewpoint, to escape from ourselves and to play a part. It can be fun for a while. It can be damaging in the end."

Any successful examination of your job or career must begin with this conscious evaluation. What is your role, as opposed to just your job? What do people see in you, both positive and negative, that makes that role appropriate? What do you like or enjoy about it? What is that fragment of who you are as a whole person that the role seems to capture (if there is one)? What is limiting about the role—how does it limit or prevent you from expressing other important aspects of yourself? Are you willing consciously to make changes so that expression can take place? What does the future look like in this job or career if you fail to do that? What happens if the organization or your coworkers cannot accept those changes?

Even more important to your understanding of self-in-career may be this question: To what extent have you defined *yourself*, or allowed yourself to be defined, by the confines of that role? Has that role come so to define you that if it were suddenly taken away from you tomorrow, you would lose the primary criterion of your value and worth?

If you are worried about the answers to those questions, you have a significant amount of inner work to do before you can make reasoned choices about your vocation. Your view of yourself is simply too small.

As much as the collective organization seems to foist upon us a role to play, there is an equal and opposite dynamic by which the individual places upon the corporation a role that he or she needs for *it* to play. This happens through a simple but profoundly important psychological dynamic known as projection. This dynamic will be revisited in the next chapter to help us understand the choices around relationships and romantic love. For now, a short version will suffice.

Any strong emotion of which we are not consciously aware (that is, unconscious) tends to be projected outwardly onto some external person, place, or thing so we can set up a relationship with that person, place, or thing that suits our needs. Most of us have, in varying degrees, strong internal needs for a sense of place, of belonging, of attachment, and it is perfectly natural for some quantum of that need to be projected onto the organizations where we work.

This accounts in no small measure for the "high" we experience right after joining a company or institution, which can last for months or even years thereafter. Think of the times in your own career when you've wanted to show off your new office to your family, or felt personal pride when the CEO remembered your name, or felt an uncommon sense of belonging when that corporate parking space opened up. It wasn't the office or the parking space or the recognition so much as what they represented to you. The very human need to identify with and feel a part of a group, once met by your family of origin but then projected progressively outward to playmates, peer groups, cliques and teams, now comes to rest upon an organization. You are proud to be an IBM'er, or a Ciscolian, or a Gulfstreamer.

Jung called such a state of unconscious identification with a group *participation mystique,* and as long as things go well in one's career, it is as harmless as it is universal. But when it comes time for an important choice respecting our jobs and careers, it can be a significant impediment. We may, as we have said, so identify ourselves with an organizational role that we find ourselves rudderless without it. Or there may be people within the organization who provide a "hook" for our projections and have either a strongly positive or strongly negative effect on us, such as the manager who unconsciously reminds us so much of a beloved parent that we are reluctant to lose such a mentor, or the coworker who reconnects us to such long-forgotten sibling rivalry that we can't wait to get the heck away from him.

But the most common impediment to clarity of consciousness may be our projections onto the organization itself. That "family"—and there are still many companies that refer to themselves in that way—will be subject to the projection of all the particularities and peculiarities of our relationship to our original family of origin and other early associations. We may stay in a situation we ought to leave because of a deeply seated if misplaced desire to maintain a sense of belonging and attachment. We may choose to leave when we should consider staying because we see the organization as suffocating and stifling of our independence. We may, alternately over time, come to see the same institution in both ways! And to complicate matters even further, just as psychologists tell us that we will often cling to patterns we know to be unhealthy just because they are familiar, we may stay in a crazy-making corporate environment because it feels strangely like home!

Projections are always tricky business, in work as well as in love, for precisely the reason that they originate in our unconscious selves. So what is the solution? "When a projection drops away from a person or organization," says Murray Stein, "they become much less important, fascinating, repugnant, or emotionally stimulating. The emotional situation is neutralized, and one realizes, 'Aha, so that is what was going on!' The projection can now be contained mentally, in conscious understanding."

In my experience, that "aha" moment does not happen quickly. It can take considerable time to parse through your feelings about your job, company, and coworkers to determine what positive and negative qualities actually belong to them and which have been thrust upon them by you. It takes insight and honesty. Sometimes, unfortunately, it may take repetitions of the same patterns and mistakes until you gain the consciousness necessary to make those distinctions. But they are essential to choices made "well enough."

THE "SECRET SAUCE" OF CAREER DECISIONS

If our assumed organizational roles and projections keep us from seeing our current employment situations clearly, what is the "secret sauce" that can help us make job and career choices more rationally? In study after study of middle-aged populations, we see a surprisingly high degree of dissatisfaction with their career choices. In my own chosen profession—the law—that figure was 41 percent in one survey. As one researcher points out, if midlife is a time for examining and revising one's sense of identity, and work roles strongly influence that identity, it is logical that we would question both at the same time.

But when asked what they would rather be doing, the answers were quite enlightening. Yes, they were very diverse: teacher, writer, artist, artisan, nurseryman, farmer, day trader, forest ranger, social worker or other profession in direct contact with those in need. But out of those disparate answers (and many more like them), a pattern emerges. No one wants to feel that he or she is a cog in a wheel of a large impersonal organization, doing meaningless work for faceless individuals, regardless of how successful the person might be at it or how much money is made doing it. Instead, when you look at each of those answers, you see a version of what could best be called *creativity*.

Now, don't be trapped by the conventional notion that only people involved in the fine arts are creative. The teacher possesses that quality just as strongly when he or she imparts something of lasting value to a student; the farmer when he fosters the endless creativity of the earth; the day trader when her research and wits pay off in profits; or the social worker when he creates new hope for a broken family. We exercise our creativity *any time we utilize our skills, knowledge, and talents to bring forth something new, to improve something extant, or to participate in the natural rhythms and cycles of the world around us.*

And by that definition, there is no reason work in a corporation or other organization cannot be creative as well. Could you apply that definition to the product or project upon which you are currently working and see that you are making a creative contribution? Could you apply it to your role as a manager and see how you are creatively affecting others and their careers? Could you apply it to the work of your team and realize that every time its output exceeds that which would have been possible from any given individual, you have just succeeded in an act of creation? And if, even after these prompts, you are unable to see "everyday creativity" in the work you do, can you not see the opportunity in the way you act and interact with those around you in the workplace?

From cog to creator: that's the special sauce. That's the movement that seems to drive practically every person who harbors significant questions about whether a particular job or career is "right" for him or her. Those questions know no particular time of life; they are not the province of any particular foundational shift. Nor is there any one "right answer" when faced with such a choice. There are, however, right *questions*, as the three true stories that follow will illustrate.

KEITH HAMILTON

For Keith Hamilton, the choice was to leave. By age fifty, he was in the position to which he had always aspired—head of research and development for an international consumer products company. And if he could have continued unfettered to use his sharp intellect and inquisitive creativity in the development of new products, he might still be in that role today. But the closer he got to the executive suite, the more this self-professed "country boy" from the hills of Oklahoma found himself struggling. "There's a certain amount of fitting in and molding yourself to the expectations of others that just has to happen. It's part of the deal and you accept it. I stayed connected to myself and my roots by getting out in the woods and hunting. My core values and motivations seem to have always been around the land and a sense of place, even though I very much enjoyed my work in science and research. I managed to keep that balance up for probably twenty years, and it worked okay for me."

But at age fifty-three, Keith was being asked to remold himself yet again, this time into the image of the new CEO of the company. And it was the CEO himself—urbane, dashing, a lover of race cars and mountain climbing—who was setting those expectations: "Be more aggressive." "Take charge and make decisions rather than relying on consensus." "Carry yourself more upright." "Dress more upscale." "Do something about that hair!"

Keith reflects back on those days in this way: "In effect, I was being asked to give up part of who I authentically was in order to fit a certain image, a role I was supposed to play. After about a year of that, I realized the pressure to conform was bleeding off my creativity as well. My heart just wasn't in it anymore. It was time to go."

And go he did. Like Charles, whom we met in our first chapter, Keith found that he could only be true to his values and his dream for himself by leaving the corporate world. Now he and his wife have, to use his words, "been adopted by" three hundred acres of land in the rolling hills of his native eastern Oklahoma. "My coworkers now are a bunch of deer and wild turkeys, and my office is the woods and fields around here. And believe you me, I'm in the office every day!"

MIKE KING

For Mike King, the choice was to make a change. A highly trained chemical engineer for an international drug giant, Mike could be something of a study in midlife development. A triathlete, he was an amazing physical specimen for a man in his forties, and his intellect and project-planning skills continued to provide success at work, inching him along an upward path in a huge corporate hierarchy. But inside he was a mess. Because of a mismatch between his innate personality and the demands of his particular job, Mike spent much of his time mired in details, worried about those details, and spending valuable energy trying in vain to control all of those details. "I'd wake up in the middle of the night worried about some fairly insignificant thing related to work," he said, "and then I'd lie awake worrying about why I was worrying so much."

The obsessiveness and pressure he was feeling about his projects at work began to spill over into his home life as well, and he and his wife began to experience a level of discord they had not known before. "I felt like things were pressing in on me from all sides. The more complex the projects that came my way, the more awash in their details I got, and the more fixated I became. The more fixated I was, the greater my troubles were at home. I began to have really serious questions about my chosen career."

But it was then that Mike took on the greatest project he would ever manage—himself. He began to read books that helped him to understand the disconnect between his personality and his particular job. He hired an executive coach and took psychometric instruments that helped him sort through his makeup, strengths, and weaknesses. In the end, he fashioned a bold project plan—complete with benchmarks, timetables, and deliverables—for his transition to another part of the company where his strengths could be better utilized, and then for leaving the company completely at age fifty-five.

"How can we live so long within ourselves," he asks, "seemingly unaware of any conflict, and then an event or confluence of events can raise our level of awareness so rapidly that we acknowledge the incongruities we did not realize just yesterday? I mean, to the rest of the world it probably appeared that everything was going well for me. It certainly seemed that way to my wife. But here I was in this huge organization, worried to death about my little tiny piece of it, all the while ignoring some talents and gifts I have that would be enlivening for me to use and might do other people some good."

When last I spoke with Mike, he had gone back to school with the intent of gaining a master's degree in psychology. The "project plan" called for him to step out of corporate life at age fifty-five ("Just when life starts to make sense," he says) and start a practice in clinical psychology.

"We are becoming accustomed to the idea of serial marriages," Gail Sheehy observes. "It will be progress when we come to think of serial careers not as signifying failure, but as a realistic way to prolong vitality." That is certainly the case with Mike King, who looks forward to channeling his considerable physical energy and intellectual curiosity into a completely new vocation.

GARY KENDALL

In his instructive little book *The Dip*, Seth Godin explores the dilemma of "when to quit and when to stick" in your current job or career. "The opposite of quitting is not 'waiting around,'" he says, "No, the opposite of quitting is *rededication*. The opposite of quitting is an invigorated new strategy designed to break the problem apart." That was the solution Gary Kendall found and embraced.

Systems engineer and project manager for a major defense contractor, Gary had watched as his career slowly slipped from star performer to sideline sub. "Project planning and organization always came naturally to me," he recalled, "but I always struggled with the political aspects of high-profile initiatives in a large entrenched culture. That was my downfall."

After decades of cost-plus aerospace contracts, where the government paid for cost overruns, Gary was placed in charge of one of the first projects in his division awarded on a "cost-plus-incentive-fee" basis. If cost overruns occurred, his company would lose money. "The company's culture was not ready to worry too much about overruns and I was too green to realize it. What's more, I was trying to apply some very cutting-edge PM [project management] processes that required the use of integrated product teams rather than stove-piped functional teams. The culture wasn't ready for this either. Those old functional managers refused to let me build cross-functional teams. I was trying to swim upstream in a very large and strong river, and I didn't even know how to swim. It was the first really serious failure of my professional life."

At age forty-four, Gary found himself demoted and shunted off to a corner office to lick his wounds. But it was then that fate, his experience, and his prior hard work combined to "break the problem apart" and give him a new sense of enthusiasm and dedication for his work.

To help him "save a little face," as he puts it, the company gave Gary a small budget and some minor responsibilities in the wake of his career setback. But Gary wasn't "waiting around" for the other shoe to drop. "I distinctly remember being at work on a Sunday afternoon a month after my demotion," he recalls, "and feeling a strong need to make something good come out of this experience. I started to develop the outline of a process for estimating the true work content that would be required by a project so that the situation I had fallen into could be avoided by others in the future. I really became dedicated to changing a system that was hard-wired for failure by uncovering and removing some of the traps that were built into the way we approached projects. I don't think I ever expected to make an impact beyond the programs that would involve me in the future."

But Gary underestimated the consequences of his rededication to his craft and the use of his creativity. The process he created continued to mature over the ensuing months and years. It was used first in Gary's next assignment when it helped a customer reclaim a significant amount of lost profit. It became widely used in his division, and then, with the support and sponsorship of Gary's boss, in all divisions within the company.

Gary says, "On a personal level this expanded my universe from a few sites around the country to most of our domestic and international facilities as well. The prospect of providing service within my area of specialty has now grown exponentially."

Just a few months prior to this writing, Gary's persistence and dedication found its reward. He was asked by the executive team to roll out a new initiative, based primarily on the processes he had developed, to assist program managers in the planning and start-up of all new company programs. In essence, he was being asked to rewire the system that had earlier in his career caused him to fail and to set up the company's new generation of managers for greater success. It would be difficult to imagine a position for which Gary was better suited, or that anyone other than Gary could do as well.

Gary reflects on his career story in this way: "There is no way I could have envisioned this, sitting in that barren little office after my downfall. I'm excited about my work again. Just a few years ago I was a broken man looking for a place to hide out until I could retire. But I look back on that time now and realize that I avoided two mistakes I could have made. I could have just sat there, waiting for the company to either throw me a bone or fire me, or I could have quit. But something told me to give it another good solid shot. I could see a need and I knew I could fill that need; and I honestly thought I had a creative perspective on the problem that no one else had, just because they were too cozy with the problem to see it. Failure can be a great teacher in that way. I believe that most of my career has been a means of preparation for this new role and I'm really glad I stuck it out."

THE VOICES

But then there are the voices. We know them all too well, don't we? They will be there to one degree or another anytime there is a weighty choice to be made or challenge to be met in our lives. They are like the Four Horsemen of our inner landscape. They are too powerful to be ignored and must be given their due consideration, but they also have the power to pull us away from life and leave us mired in the muck of indecision. They are the voices of Vanity, Obligation, Security, and "Reality." (The word is in quotes because, at least to some extent, reality is perception and perception is individual.)

The voice of Vanity is simply the concern about what others will think. *Won't people assume I failed? Doesn't this look like a step backward? What will my family make of this?* While our concern is understandable, we must recognize that those questions come from the vanity of our own egos. We are not so much concerned, per se, with what other people think or how they feel; we're more concerned with how those thoughts or feelings affect *us* and our own image of ourselves. If that self-image is tied too closely to our current organizational role or job, then any significant change becomes impossible. The options from which we can choose are narrowed to only those which will seem to *others* to be straight-line progression along a defined career path.

The reader drawn to that siren song would be well-served by revisiting our first chapter and the tasks of the first foundational shift (specifically, becoming one's own person) or exploring in the next chapter the choices we make about our most important relationships.

The voice of Obligation is a different matter. There are people who depend on us. When we are first starting a family, that dependency is immediate and obvious, particularly if one spouse chooses to stay home or otherwise postpone part of his or her income potential. But there are also many of us in our fifties and beyond who have discovered that the legitimate needs of our children do not end when they turn twenty-one. The voice of Obligation may legitimately ask us to modify or postpone our choices in favor of the needs of others. But we must be careful not to take that logic too far. Do we serve our loved ones well by plugging away endlessly at a job or career that is no match for our abilities? What lessons do we teach our children when dull-as-dirt duty swamps our creativity? What benefit might accrue to our children's lives if they saw us at our best, both in how we love and in how we work? Choices have consequences, and they are sometimes far from immediately visible.

A cousin of Obligation is the voice of Security. As Maslow observed through his famous "hierarchy of needs," a sense of physical safety and security is a prerequisite for almost any form of human growth and development. Fortunately, the basic security from harm is not an issue for most of us. Beyond that, however, the sense of *psychological* security in our society tends to revolve around money—how much we have, how much we've saved, how much we can earn in the future. And as individuals, we differ wildly in the strength of that internal need.

The Hogan Leadership Values Profile, one of the premier instruments used by executive coaches and psychologists to measure the strength of core values and motivators, defines Security as "a need for predictability and structure, and efforts to avoid risk and uncertainty—especially in the employment area—and a lifestyle organized around minimizing errors and mistakes." As the Hogan definition implies, an unusually low score on this scale (that is, very little need for security) can result in a kind of recklessness, while unusually high scores can lead us to a tortoise-like existence where we snap our shells shut at the first sign of something new or unusual. Move too impulsively and you risk making a serious mistake; refuse to move at all and you are doomed to life-as-it-is with no possibility of parole.

What's more, it is a paradox of life in modern corporations that actively seeking security may be the most dangerous thing you can do. Companies are constantly looking for ways to cut perceived deadwood out of their organizations, and "coasters" will be the very first to go.

Sometimes the most prudent thing to do does not intuitively seem to be the safest. When a young Theodore Roosevelt was pinned down with his men on the slopes of San Juan Hill in the decisive battle of the Spanish-American War, his choices were three in number. He could sound retreat, leaving the Spaniards with possession of the high ground, but living to fight another day. He could continue to hunker down and see his men get picked off one by one by the fire from above and hope reinforcements would arrive in time. Or he could charge directly into the teeth of the Spanish position. By his reckoning, fewer American lives would be lost in this bold and unexpected move than with either of the first two choices. History will never know for sure whether he was right in that calculation, but the experience helped forge the beliefs of one of America's most dynamic political personalities and vaulted Teddy Roosevelt to national prominence.

Years later, the twenty-sixth president would express the thought this way: "In any moment of decision, the best thing you can do is the right thing, the next best thing is the wrong thing, and the worst thing you can do is nothing."

And then there is the voice of "Reality." As I stated previously, the word is in quotes because reality is perception and perception is individual. Perception is not absolute. Still, there are some things about which we can be relatively sure. Jumping off a tall building will likely do you harm. Picking up a musical instrument for the first time in your later years (as did Socrates) will not likely render you a virtuoso. And my days as a baseball player are far, far behind me. So the inner voice that says *you can't* easily chimes in with those that say *you shouldn't, you ought not,* and *what will they think?*

But be careful how narrowly you define your own reality. In this book, we have already met quite a number of people who have discovered new directions, started new ventures, challenged limiting assumptions, and otherwise reinvented their personal "reality." Don't be so sure that what seems to be is all there is.

In a most insightful article titled "The Real Reason People Won't Change," Robert Kegan and Lisa Laskow Lahey explore the reasons why the voices of Vanity, Obligation, Security, and "Reality" are, at least some of the time, less the product of conscious logic than the result of our *unconscious* fears and assumptions. The basic idea is that while almost all of us are consciously committed to making the most of our lives and to making the changes necessary to accomplish that, we are often struggling unconsciously with an opposing agenda, which the authors aptly call a "competing commitment." Discovering the competing commitment will not make it go away, nor necessarily should it, but it allows us to make cleaner choices that are less contaminated by our unknown fears and assumptions.

Allow me to use myself and this book as an example. For years after the publication of my first book, *The Congruent Life*, I knew I wanted to write a second book about the life transitions I saw taking place in my clients, and how those transitions affected their lives and careers. I would carve out time to do research and begin this new work, only to get involved in some exciting new project that would take me away from the book for months at a time. When I would come back to it, I wasn't quite sure I liked what I had previously written, or I had developed some new insight about it, and I would scrap entire sections of the work. The pattern continued for years. I could say in all honesty that I was committed to this book and to making the changes to my life that would be necessary to birth it; but I had to conclude that something within me, which I was not fully acknowledging, was holding me back.

Here's how Kegan and Lahey would have proposed that I uncover my "competing commitment." First, I needed to ask myself, "What would you like to see changed about your work, so that you could be more effective or the work would be more satisfying?" Answers to this question almost always take the form of a complaint. For me it was, "I wish I had more time to devote to working on this book project." As Kegan and Lahey point out, "complaints can be immensely useful. People complain only about the things they care about, and they complain the loudest about the things they care about most."

Which leads to a second question: "What commitments does your complaint imply?" For me the answer to that was pretty clear. "I am committed to writing this book. I cannot *not* do it. It's as simple as that."

But then the tough part starts. We are almost always responsible, at least in part, for getting in our own way. So the third question becomes, "What are you doing, or not doing, that is keeping your commitment from being more fully realized?"

I could identify my own undermining behavior pretty easily: "I get involved in more lucrative business opportunities, and while I do enjoy that work, it keeps me away from my manuscript for way too long."

Now we're getting somewhere. Understanding the consequences of our undermining behavior, it is now important to consider what the consequences would be if we suddenly started *foregoing* the behavior. The fourth question: "If you imagine doing the opposite of the undermining behavior, do you detect in yourself any discomfort, worry, or vague fear?"

This is asking us to be aware enough of our own emotions that we can see the tire tracks left by our own unconscious competing commitment. For me, if I thought about it long enough and was honest enough with myself, I would have to say, "I would worry about foregoing so much potential income. I would also feel uncomfortable trying to explain to other people why I was taking a break from being a lawyer and consultant to be a—what? A *writer*?" (Can you recognize the clear voices of Vanity and Security here?)

Finally, our passive fears do not ordinarily remain passive; they translate into actions, even if unconscious, designed to prevent the things that we fear. So the last question is this: "By engaging in this undermining behavior, what worrisome outcome are you committed to preventing?" The answer to that question is the very face of the competing commitment. Here's mine: "I am worried I will fail, and I am more afraid of the feeling of having failed than I am of practically anything else in this life."

I could just as easily have said, with some degree of truthfulness, that I was afraid the task was beyond me (voice of "Reality"), or that I was worried about foregoing a steady income (Security), or that I was worried about shortchanging my children (Obligation), or that I was worried about what the neighbors would say to each other when they see me home every day (Vanity).

"Such revelations can feel embarrassing," say Kegan and Lahey. "While primary commitments almost always reflect noble goals that we would be happy to shout from the rooftops, competing commitments are very personal, reflecting vulnerabilities that people fear will undermine how they are regarded both by others and themselves. Little wonder people keep them hidden and hasten to cover them up again once they are on the table."

Competing commitments do not arise out of thin air. They are based on our assumptions about ourselves and the world we inhabit. If we take the time to look at them, we will often find that our assumptions come from our earliest experiences and our attempts to get along in and make sense of the world around us. I can now see clearly that my fear of failure was a natural and self-protective outgrowth of a childhood where success in traditional pursuits garnered exaggerated praise, while "disappointing" my parents was made to feel worse than any corporal punishment could ever have been. Thus my "big assumption" (to borrow again from the terminology of Kegan and Lahey) was that to try something very difficult and fail was not a learning experience or worthwhile effort but a cosmic disappointment to be avoided.

For my client Tony, a childhood in foster homes and a messy divorce in adulthood have created his big assumption that the world is a dangerous place and that people are not to be trusted until they prove clearly to the contrary. So while his primary commitment as a human resources manager is to be a trusted ally to his company's employees, his conscious desires are consistently undermined by a skepticism that serves his competing commitment to being strong and invulnerable.

Kegan and Lahey would offer this observation to both Tony and me: "Unquestioning acceptance of a big assumption anchors and sustains an immune system: A competing commitment makes all the sense in the world, and the person continues to engage in behaviors that support it, albeit unconsciously, to the detriment of his or her 'official,' stated commitment. Only by bringing big assumptions to light can people finally challenge their assumptions and recognize why they are engaging in seemingly contradictory behavior."

And, I might add, only then can they make choices that are both conscious and rational. If it were not possible to understand our big assumptions, test them out to see if they are actually true, and occasionally challenge them, this book would not exist.

SOME SUGGESTIONS

The choices around career, along with those concerning relationships, are generally the most difficult of our lives, precisely because so much is felt to be at stake. But there are a few things you can do to ensure that the choices you make about work will be "good enough" in the long run.

1. *Engage your allies.* I'm not talking about those people who will simply parrot back to you what you want to hear. Be open about

your process, your thoughts, and your feelings with those who will support *and* challenge you.

The latter is particularly important. I owe a great debt to the people in my life like Fred Harwell. In 1989, after a stint as a corporate attorney, I was considering whether to attempt a return to private law practice or to move toward academia. A successful trial lawyer and friend, Fred listened attentively across a restaurant table as I prattled on about all the things I thought I could bring to a large, traditional law firm. He finally interrupted me with a single pinprick to my balloon: "Mike, you're just not cut out for that." After the most awkward of silences, during which I actually considered getting up and walking away from the table in anger, Fred continued: "I know that's what you think you want, and I'm not saying you're not smart enough, but it's just not your personality. Somebody has to tell you that."

I will always be grateful, if grudgingly, for Fred's honesty. As it turns out, he was absolutely right.

2. *Do your homework.* Talk to as many people as you can who have made a choice similar to the one you are facing or who do the kind of work you are contemplating. Insight will come from some of the most surprising and unlikely sources.

We sometimes think people who are in positions or jobs to which we aspire won't "waste time" talking to some neophyte. My experience has been quite the opposite—people enjoy talking about what they do, and even at the highest levels of organizations they are often generous with their time for those who indicate a genuine interest and desire to learn.

3. *Be patient.* Unless there is a valid external reason for setting a time limit on your process, try not to set one. The conversations you need to have and the research you need to do will take time, and muddy waters don't easily clarify when constantly stirred. If you find yourself with an unnecessary sense of urgency about making a change, you risk acting too precipitously, which is the equal and opposite mistake of sitting around and doing nothing

at all. Acting when you should be learning and experimenting is no greater virtue than complete inaction. With the former you may succeed in changing the scenery, but the road you are traveling may be the same old dead end.

4. *Ask yourself*: "Am I making progress where I am?" In your current work life, you are either moving ahead toward your goals, hopes, and dreams; standing still; or losing ground. Those are the only three possibilities. As Seth Godin puts it:

> To succeed, to get to that light at the end of the tunnel, you've got to make some kind of forward progress, no matter how small. Too often we get stuck in a situation where quitting seems too painful, so we just stay with it, choosing not to quit because it's easier than quitting. That choice—to stick with it in the absence of forward progress, is a waste. It's a waste because of the opportunity cost—you could be doing something far better, and far more pleasurable, with your time.

Progress can be measured in any number of very personal ways. Perhaps the measurement is financial; more often it is gauged by how we are developing and growing, how much we are learning and gaining, and how much our achievements are recognized by others and by ourselves. Perhaps there are times and situations in our lives where progress is recognizable only in another mortgage or tuition payment met, and those worthy goals make our daily coal-mine existence worthwhile. Still, whatever its measure, the lack of discernable forward progress is a serious matter given that the only other options are stagnation and regression.

5. *Test your "Reality."* You may think you know what daily life is like for a lawyer or a chef or a nurse or a small-business owner. Chances are you're way off base. In addition to talking to those people who live the careers you contemplate, find ways to stick a toe or two in the water just to get a sense of how it feels. If

you aspire to teach, a local community college might well be able to use your current expertise as an adjunct instructor for a semester. If you think you're called to the clergy, try volunteering to shepherd an adult study group for a few months, or sit in on some seminary classes with the permission of the professor. If you fancy yourself a health-care professional, or engineer, or paralegal, spend a day or two "shadowing" someone who does this for a living. Be creative. There are dozens of ways to walk in someone else's shoes for a day without having to box up those shoes and take them home with you.

6. *Manage your income expectations.* There is an inverse correlation between your financial desires and your career options. The more money you think you need to be "happy" or "secure," the fewer the career choices available to you. At its logical extreme you can become the fabled bird in a gilded cage—unable to escape your self-imposed prison because you fear the sacrifices that would be necessary to gain your freedom. Don't give the voices of Obligation and Security a permanent mortgage on your life.

7. *Reframe the issue.* Speaking of the voices of Obligation and Security, it is all too easy to let them frame your job and career choices in their own familiar language. Those voices will use words such as "quitter," or say you're "getting off track," or loft up a descriptor such as "reckless." And then there's the sarcastic and degrading "He doesn't know what he wants to do when he grows up."

   Language is important, and the language used by the voices of Obligation and Security is heavily stacked in favor of the status quo. In your own self-talk and in conversations with others, it may be very important to change that balance of power. Instead of quitting, are you really talking about a new beginning? When the voices accuse you of being off track, can you insist that you are looking for a new and faster track? Instead of reckless, are you only trying to prevent a wreck further down the line? And when the inner or outer voices question your maturity, insist that you're not only a grownup but you're trying to grow into the kind of grownup you are intended to be. *Illegitimi non carborundum!* ("Don't let the bastards wear you down!")

After all, the truth is that jobs or careers are only vehicles for getting us where we'd like to go in our lives. They are not an end unto themselves. They are tactics to reach much larger goals. To change jobs or even careers for the right reasons is merely a tactical move in the saga of your life. To take one famous example, consider the career path of Abraham Lincoln. Before becoming an attorney, he managed a mill, drove a grocery store into bankruptcy, took up land surveying, was the town postmaster, did odd jobs including splitting rails, captained a militia unit, and unsuccessfully ran for public office. With the exception of the bankruptcy, which left him heavily in debt, Lincoln never expressed regret or disappointment with any of these varied career choices. Indeed, each was arguably a vehicle for preparing him for the great challenges his life held in store.

8. *Remember The Dream.* In our chapter on the third foundational shift, we explored that acorn of your individuality which we called The Dream—your earliest vision of the kind of life you wished to lead as an adult. Dreams, quite understandably, can get postponed, often in response to the compelling voices of Obligation and "Reality." But The Dream postponed will not often remain denied and will usually resurface at important junctures in our lives. In times of crucial decisions about work and career, the dream had best be given its due.

Don't know how to spot The Dream? Have you forgotten what it looks like? Then some deep reflection on the following questions might be helpful to you.

- What were your first clear ideas of what you wanted to do with your life? Why did that appeal to you?
- If you have had changes in your career aspirations over the years, when did that happen and what was the "pull" on you?

- Did you ever have a job that made you eager to get out of bed and go to work? Why was that? What skills and talents did you use? Was the work itself important to you, or were there other reasons for your eagerness?
- If you could put together the elements of an ideal job, what would they be? Why?
- Assume you were asked to create a position for yourself that you could do better than anyone else you know—maybe better than anyone else on Earth. No one else could do this particular thing quite as well as you because you brought something unique to the task. What would that position be? What would make you so uniquely qualified?
- Finally, if someone offered you enough money so that you did not have to work again and would be financially comfortable, would you retire or continue working? If the former, what would you want to do with your productive time? If the latter, what kind of work would you choose?

Reflections on these questions will provide hints and showings of your original personal Dream. It may be time for you to at least incline your career choices toward the kinds of values, talents, and purposes The Dream represents. To the extent that you can do that, you at least assure yourself of work that is fun, personally satisfying, and aligned with your talents and gifts. Besides, the inner truth The Dream represents is not likely to forever allow itself to be drowned out by the voices of Obligation and "Reality." You might as well begin to cooperate.

Choices II:
Love, Marriage, and Relationships

Life does not give itself to one who tries to keep all of its advantages at once. I have often thought morality may perhaps consist solely in the courage of making a choice.—Leon Blum

All growth is costly. It involves the leaving behind of an old way of being in the world. Often it involves, at least for a time, leaving behind the others who have been identified with that old way of being.—Robert Kegan

LIFE SAVES ITS THORNIEST issues and dilemmas for the realm of our most intimate relationships. Sexuality, love, and marriage have always probed the furthest limits of our humanity, forging our strongest qualities even as they expose our most pitiable weaknesses. No one gets a hall pass from the great, wonderful learning experience that is a lifetime of evolving relationships.

A book about the principal foundational shifts in life could not do justice to the full complexities of human relationships. Yet choices regarding those relationships are often at the very epicenter of the seismic shifts that take place in our lives and are thus deserving of our fullest attention, particularly in the maelstrom that often accompanies the second (midlife) shift. Our choices around relationships may, in fact, eclipse all others, and determine whether that critical transition is safely and successfully navigated.

ROMANCE

The reasons for spousal infidelity may outnumber the stars. One man starts to sense a bodily decline in midlife and wants to see himself again handsome and strong through the eyes of a new lover. A woman in the throes of the first foundational shift wants to reassert her selfhood after years of emotional abuse. A man in his fifties may tell himself that this is his "last chance" for an affair. A woman in her forties seeks unconsciously to be "found out" so she can blow a stale marriage wide open. Some people simply need a bridge out of their current situation, and this is the easiest way to build one.

But the biggest single reason for infidelities during life's transitions has nothing to do with fear, or revenge, or boredom, or dissatisfaction, or even the emotional and physical pleasures of sexuality. Instead, it has everything to do with the universal psychological phenomenon of projection (first discussed in the preceding chapter) and its connection to the intense emotions we call romantic love.

To quote Robert Johnson, author of *We: Understanding the Psychology of Romantic Love:*

> We know there is something inexplicable in romance. When we look at the feelings that rampage through us, we know that it is not just companionship or sexual attraction, and it is not that quiet, devoted, unromantic love that we often see in stable marriages and relationships. It is something more, something different.
>
> When we are "in love" we feel completed, as though a missing part of ourselves had been returned to us; we feel uplifted, as though we were suddenly raised above the level of the ordinary world. Life has an intensity, a glory, an ecstasy and transcendence.
>
> We seek in romantic love to be possessed by our love, to soar to the heights, to find ultimate meaning and fulfillment in our beloved. We seek the feeling of wholeness.
>
> Why the "feeling of wholeness"? What is it about this thing we call romantic or idealized love that has the power to remove us from the

fractured banality of life-as-it-is and lift us up to a feeling of completion and transcendence, soaring with the eagles above?

I need to acknowledge at this point that in working with clients who are in the grips of this dynamic, I either feel like I am preaching to the choir or to total unbelievers. They either "get it," at least intellectually, because they have seen the drama unfold a sufficient number of times in their own lives or those of their friends. Or they simply refuse to look at it, because as far as they are concerned, no one, nowhere, at no time in human history has ever experienced the depth or profundity of what they are feeling, and there is certainly no one else on earth quite like the person they are in love with.

But both the choir and the unbelievers will need to consciously understand the dynamic of romantic love and deploy that understanding on the ground, as it were, in their lives, or they will forever remain the loyal subjects of an unconscious process whose causes they do not understand and whose effects they veritably worship.

While no age is immune to this dynamic, it is helpful to think back to the first time(s) in adolescence or early adulthood when you truly felt yourself to be "in love." Remember the endless daydreams, the fantasies about the future, the infatuation, the inability to do anything else but eat, sleep, think, and dream this newfound love. But think too about the superlatives you would use to describe him or her. To the rest of the world this person may have been ugly as a stick and as dumb as a rock, but to you, he or she was the most, the best, the greatest, the highest—and eternally so.

Think too about the endless conversations with the beloved. How many hours were spent talking (or, these days, texting) about likes and dislikes, hopes and dreams, accomplishments real or embellished, qualities possessed or aspired to. For probably the first time in your life it felt important, vitally important, to be deeply revealing—who you were and wanted to be—and to have the other affirm you.

As wondrous as this process is—and, lest we forget, necessary for the procreation of the species—it owes its existence to a bit of a psychological trick. Each of us enters adolescence (some would say life itself) with an image that is both *idealized* and *unconscious* of what that perfect member of the opposite sex should be like. Jung chose the word "anima" to represent the female image inherent in a man. It comes from the Latin word for "soul" but could also be translated as "she who animates." The male image resident inside a woman Jung called the "animus," which means "spirit."

Such otherworldly terms were chosen by Jung to remind us that the images are not of a particular flesh-and-blood man or woman but are internal and generalized patterns that are part of our unconscious makeup. To Jung, the anima and animus were but two examples of what he called "archetypes" (from the Greek words meaning "first model" or "original pattern"). Like my fingerprint, my anima image will be anywhere from slightly different to wildly divergent from that of another man, and the same can be said of a woman's animus. And interestingly—perhaps strangely—that image will be largely unaffected by hereditary or environmental effects.

This nice little schema quickly goes from theory to practice as soon as you meet someone who touches upon that image for you. The inner scene now set, enter stage left the universal human phenomenon of projection.

It is a psychological axiom that all things which are unconscious within us are projected outward. Because we are not consciously aware of them, the only way we can recognize and deal with our hidden thoughts, feelings, needs, and fears is to see them manifested outside of us. As unconscious as our inner images of the opposite sex may be, those projections come out of us like buckshot as soon as we begin to locate suitable targets around us.

Our aim is far from indiscriminate. The target of our newfound affection will almost always have some suitable "hook" upon which to hang our projections. He or she reminds us, in ways that hint of miracle and mystery, of that unknown inner form which we hold so dear and sacred. "That's why," James Hillman observes, "love is so overwhelming. It knocks your socks off as it lifts you right out of your shoes, and out of this world."

But here is the trick. Because projection is inside out, the qualities and traits with which we imbue our beloved really belong to us; *and* because we tend to project those aspects of ourselves of which we are most unconscious, they tend to be those qualities and traits that are most underdeveloped. So a woman who is by nature strongly self-assertive and brassily confident may find herself attracted to a man who conveys a gentle warmth and vulnerability—to the amazement of her friends. What those friends don't realize (or, perhaps, she) is that aspects of the man's personality provide convenient hooks for her to hang the projected qualities she would do well to develop in herself—qualities consistent with an animus image that looks a bit like the "strong, silent type."

On the other hand, a man who is reflective but somewhat reticent around others might gravitate toward a woman who is physically striking and socially fluid, secretly asking this earthly anima to both mirror back to him and affirm him in his perceived strengths, and accept his projections of those qualities he would so love to emulate. The old bromide about opposites attracting can now be seen in a new light.

Thank God for romantic love. As the old song says, it truly makes the world go 'round. Let nothing on these pages dissuade you from falling into its arms or from rejoicing when friends or children are swept into its ethereal realm.

The problem is that idealized love does not last, as anyone who has been in a truly long-term relationship will attest. It's not even meant to. That statement may seem like heresy to our modern culture. From pulp novels to the silver screen to the TV show *Inside Edition*, we are presented images of love and marriage that have everything to do with a romantic, magical ideal and very little to do with real-life human experience.

Popular music, as much as we all love it, is probably the worst offender. In fact, if you took all of the love songs of the last fifty years and condensed them into one, its lyrics might go something like this:

I was worthless blown debris
Until the day that I met Thee
You lifted me and made me whole
And pitched a tent within my soul

Like a vision from above
You came and captured all my love
And no one past, and no one new
Could ever change my love for You

But now you're gone. I don't know why
And I'm so lonesome I could cry
And I will never love again
Until that date with your best friend
    Next week.

Throughout adolescence and young adulthood, we will burn a path through many such love songs and look into many a face in search of the ideal one who can mirror back to us what we so need to see, all the while blissfully unaware of the psychological dynamic that fuels our search. It should be so. When we are emerging from family and other systems that surround us in our youth, we are rife for the development of all sorts of new potentialities within us. And many of those possibilities are so hidden from us, so unconscious to us, that we can only see them when they are projected outward onto another person.

As Robert Johnson puts it, "A part of us which has been hidden is about to emerge, but it doesn't go in a straight line from the unconscious to consciouness. It travels by way of an intermediary. We project our developing potential onto someone, and suddenly we're consumed with him or her. The first inkling that something in us is attempting to change is when we see another person sparkle for us."

And who among us does not remember what that "sparkle" was like? We were willingly and completely possessed by our anima/animus, which was aided in its task by a veritable flood of hormones and chemicals that increased our sense of well-being and fixated our focus on the beloved. But that state of hyper-sense was not infinitely sustainable and never could be. It's a little like being thrilled when lightning illuminates the sky but then wishing it could remain our sole source of light. That task is best carried out by an ordinary, reliable fluorescent bulb.

We were made—designed if you will—to fall in love. We learn, grow, procreate, and participate in some way in the divine mystery of life. But we were never built to be able to endlessly sustain the rapturous intensity of romantic love any more than a bolt of lightning is a sustainable form of energy.

Our cultural definition of love is harmful in two ways. It perpetuates, long after its natural emergence in adolescence and young adulthood, a system based in large part on projection and myth. We can burden our partners with expectations that are not realistic and with needs which can never be fully met by another human being. It can obscure, at least in part, the reality of the flesh-and-blood person with whom we are in relationship. And it keeps us from recognizing that what we are projecting outward belongs to *us,* whether in the form of baggage we should be opening and cleaning out ourselves or unrecognized potential we seek to live through our partner.

But the second way the cultural definition causes harm is even more pernicious. It leads to the presumption that if "the thrill is gone," if we've lost some of our intensity, then the relationship is no longer living up to the ideal. It's time to find a new relationship.

"We assume," says Johnson, "that the single ingredient we need for 'relationship,' the one thing it cannot do without, is romance. But in fact, the essential ingredients for relationship are affection and commitment. If we look clearly, we begin to see that romance is a completely different energy system, a completely distinct set of values, from love and commitment."

If we want romance, then we can find it, but we will likely continue the cycle of gaining it, losing it, and finding it again, like an eternal adolescent, for the rest of our days. If we instead want a relationship that can be a source of light and warmth even when we are no longer on fire with passion, we will need to allow the withdrawal of our projections and check our tendency to idealize our partner.

But it's often not that easy. As our lives move past adolescence and young adulthood, the pull of romantic love and the power of our anima/animus projections remain strong. Is it possible that at other important shift points in our lives, where new possibilities are emerging and new aspects of ourselves are becoming conscious, we might again fall under the spell of those powerful forces? Now, that was a stupid question, wasn't it?

Gary and Mike Redux

In the previous chapter I introduced you to Gary Kendall and Mike King. Gary, a project manager for a large aerospace company, found new energy and vitality in his work at the end of a midlife transition and recommitted to his job. Mike, a chemical engineer with an international drug company, used his foundational shift as a springboard to a new and, for him, more satisfying career. Different people, different choices.

What they shared, however, was the onset of an experience to which they thought the years had made them immune—they fell in love. "Just when I thought things had leveled out in my life," Gary recalls, "I accepted a request to mentor a new high-potential employee named Ginger who was just learning the ropes of our craft. She had been through a messy divorce two years earlier, and I, of course, had been very happily married to Debbie since about the time the continents split apart.

"But my parents had divorced when I was a teenager, so I had a lot of empathy for anyone in that situation. Once Ginger and I started talking about it, it's as if some trap door had sprung open for both of us. It seems like we talked all the time.

"While all that was going on, Deb and I really weren't spending much time together. We lived in a suburb of LA and she had a 30 mile commute in one direction and I had a 20 mile commute in the other. Our friends were mostly the people we worked with.

"It wasn't long before the character of the conversations I was having with Ginger began to change. I talked about my career and personal frustrations; she talked about her love life—or lack thereof. Looking back, I knew I was on a slippery slope even then, but it just felt too good to stop. I was drawn like a moth to a flame. It got to the point that I couldn't even take a trip with Deb without thinking about emailing or calling my coworker. And the thoughts were beginning to turn adulterous."

At precisely that point, however, two events intervened. Debbie was diagnosed with breast cancer and required months of treatments to recover. And Gary's mentee fell head over heels for another coworker, whom she subsequently married.

"What that year allowed me to do was to reconnect with my feelings for Deb and to discover some new ones," Gary says. "I saw her more for who she was rather than just her role in my life—a role I'd come to take for granted. I saw Ginger more clearly as well; and for all of her wonderful qualities, I know we could never have made a go of it in the long term. I call it my 'emotional affair' because it never became sexual. But it did have all those exciting feelings of being in love. I'm happy for her that she's found what she needs, and I'll always be grateful for the way she burst me open like a pomegranate and of helped me pick through those seeds. Some were sour, some were sweet, but all of them needed to be tasted by me."

For Mike, the story had a different ending. His wife could never accept the fact that the ground was shifting underneath him or that he, in his own words, "had to move forward or rot where I stood." She just wasn't in the same place or feeling the same seismic pressures and felt personally threatened by what was happening inside Mike. Grapes do not ripen in the same season as the strawberries.

After two agonizing years of trying to save his marriage while persevering in his own personal growth, Mike met a young psychologist named Anne. "For the first time in a very long while I felt like I had a companion; I had support; I had understanding. And I could give as good as I got. There was a kind of electrical charge between us that is very hard to describe. We were inseparable from day one."

Mike's marriage ended in divorce: "About as amicable a one as you could have under the circumstances," he reports. He now lives with Anne and her teenage children.

The roads taken by Mike and Gary were very different, but there were common waysides they shared with a great many other men and women—far more than you might guess.

In today's Western society, we marry out of love rather than through family agreement or parental arrangements. We are thus "bedfellows" from the beginning with some degree of the romantic ideal. We "fall in love," investing our mates with numinous powers while shackling them to our heaviest burdens. We expect them to complete us and meet our deepest needs while staunching our wounds and protecting our most tender places.

It is a tall order—and unrealistic. It does not hold up well in and of itself in the ensuing months and years of crying babies, money worries, work obligations, weariness, cleaning up dog poop, and the thousand different realities of what a young friend of mine calls "the assault years."

Inevitably (some therapists say as quickly as six months), the varnish begins to dull, the paint begins to peel, and we begin to see this person whom we married for all the things he or she truly is rather than for what he or she can do for us. In the language of psychology, we begin to withdraw our projections. Within this process grow the seeds of what Jung called the "dangerous age." He was referring specifically to the midlife transition, but we now know that the changes afoot in either of the three foundational shifts can prompt a reassessment or reconfiguration of the marital relationship.

A man may realize his marriage was flawed from the outset and that he stayed in it for as long as he did because of children, finances, family pressures, or simple inertia. A woman may realize that despite living in the same house for a good many years—perhaps even raising children together—she and her husband share practically no interests, friends, values, or concerns. In the midst of a foundational shift, a kind of veil may be lifted, and either of them may see how profoundly unsatisfying their marriage has become.

For either, the stage is now perfectly set for the reemergence of romantic love. Unconsciously scanning the horizon of their daily interactions, their anima/animus projections are seeking just the right person and circumstance upon which to alight. With uncommon frequency, the darts of their projections will find their marks, and in due time they will be filled with the same kind of fitful longing that had once been directed toward their mate, accompanied by an unshakable belief that this new love will be and will provide all the things their mate could not.

It is truly astounding how often variations on this theme are played and replayed in the lives of modern people. Fortunately, the stories do not always end badly. For Gary, the opportunity for withdrawal of projections which was foisted upon him by his wife's illness led to a deeper and richer kind of love—less idealized and more authentic. For Mike, the second time was the charm, leading him from the depths of depression to the upslope of self-discovery and finally to the plateau of a happier and more productive life.

Unfortunately, it seems that for every Mike or Gary, there is another soul who stays mired in a stagnant or destructive marriage, or for whom the "breakout" of a new anima/animus projection is but the first of many repetitions of the same pattern, sometimes lasting the rest of their lives. The mate changes but the pattern remains, at great cost to the people and families affected. For either, it can be said that they do not simply have an anima or an animus—it has *them*.

It is only through consciousness and choice—*conscious choice*—that we navigate the often turbulent waters around love, marriage, and relationship. Robert Johnson puts it starkly: "The love potion is strong: The new morality of romance is deeply ingrained in us; it seizes us and dominates us when we least expect it. To put the love potion on the correct level, to live it without betraying his human relationships, is the most difficult task of consciousness that any man can undertake in our modern Western world."

THE PATTERN OF OUR PROJECTIONS

Conscious of what? First and foremost, you must be sufficiently aware of the pattern of your own projection so you will know it when you see it. Being a student of your own history and not only of your romantic past is invaluable here. If you look carefully, you will see the same dynamic in operation anytime you have enjoyed an inexplicable fascination with a person (a positive projection) or anytime you have endured an intense dislike for another (negative projection).

The first stage of projection we have already discussed: our inner needs, potentialities, and ideals are projected from the inside out. In the case of romantic love, the object of our affection embodies for us that image of near perfection. The faults of our beloved, which may be all too obvious to the rest of the world, are invisible to us, and we load onto him or her all the needs and expectations that would befit this perfect mate.

But then, in a usually gradual process called "integration," we begin to see more clearly the differences between the projected image and the reality of the other person. His or her feet are capable, as it were, of smelling just as bad as anyone else's. He or she has a past, has made mistakes, has limitations, has idiosyncrasies, has a life apart from yours.

The crucial third stage, where we bring those discrepancies to the light of consciousness and are able to see them as the illusions they always were, is the critical moment in any relationship. If we are lacking in consciousness and maturity, we may conclude that we were simply wrong in choosing this particular person, break off the relationship, and embark on a new search for that ideal mate without really noticing all the positive qualities possessed by the person we just left behind—because he or she didn't meet our needs.

Worse yet, when our expectations are frustrated, our projections onto the other can quickly flip from the positive to the negative. This is the thin line between love and hate to which any family therapist or divorce lawyer can attest. Passionate love can become equally passionate hatred. In either event, we fail to become conscious of our projections and continue our unconscious insistence that our perfect beloved perfectly meet our infantile needs.

Such dangerous pitfalls indicate why the last stage of the process of integration is so important. Having withdrawn our projections and faced squarely the differences between our illusions and reality, we must turn inward once again: we must look within ourselves to understand why our particular anima/animus images were as they were in the first place. Why did we expect our husband to be the ultimate guardian and protector yet feel stifled when he exercised too much control over family finances? Why did we like our wife to be feminine and demure in public but become angry when she wasn't more aggressive in bargaining with that car salesman? What were the roles we expected of each other when it came to sex, work, child-rearing, finances, chores, et al.?

Of one thing we can be sure: each of those needs, each of those expectations, and each of our ideals about how things "should" be in our relationships originated inside of us. While it is hard, often backbreaking work to unearth those inner origins, it is critical to the concept of conscious choice in our relationships. Without it, you will continue to repeat your patterns ad infinitum—or worse still, watch your once-positive projections flip to the negative.

But if we stick with that inner work of consciousness, we will find it capable of paying some very substantial dividends. We could, for example, find that being "dis-illusioned" is not such a bad thing when it allows us to see more clearly the lovable and admirable human qualities our partners do in fact possess. The kind of devoted and committed love that grows and deepens with the years begins by seeing past our illusions and into the essence of the other.

Moreover, we get a shot at taking responsibility for our own satisfaction in life. To be aware of the origin of our needs, hopes, and expectations about life is to take ownership of them. We can no longer get away with expecting our mate to do all of our heavy lifting for us or blaming him or her for not keeping us satisfied.

The idealized other, whom we hoped would take care of us, meet all our needs, and always be there for us no matter what is seen as an ordinary person with the same caliber of needs and expectations as our own. They are our mate—not God, nor even an all-loving parent. Integration and the withdrawal of projections invites us to be adults.

DIFFERING TIMELINES

A second act of consciousness, essential for any man or woman in a long–term, committed relationship, is to realize that partners rarely experience the same foundational shift at precisely the same time. As Roger Gould points out in his book *Transformations*, a partner who is enjoying the relative comfort (we called it embeddedness in the introduction) of being between transitions may feel a certain "developmental envy" toward the partner who is on the upslope of change. In my experience, the emotion is less envy than fear of the future, of the unknown, of a process that feels quite foreign because it has not yet been experienced.

On the other side of the marriage, Gould observes, "There may be surface peace, but the building internal tension finally bursts forth from the partner who is more alienated, lonely, or more deprived of the opportunity to deal with his/her inner needs."

Again, in my experience, the partner who is a little ahead of the curve can display a certain hubris and self-righteousness, as if the changes taking place within him or her have bestowed some special knowledge, and he or she is being "held back" by the other from acting on it.

Jung had an interesting way of looking at the developmental disparity between partners in a marriage. He described it as "the problem of the 'contained' and 'container.'" To Jung, it was obvious that, "Even the best of marriages cannot expunge individual differences so completely that the state of mind of the partners is absolutely identical." Thus, the movement toward fundamental change "does not begin simultaneously for both parties."

The partner who is "contained" feels himself to be living more or less within the confines of the marriage, and his or her projection onto the container/mate is more or less complete. For the contained mate, this is a quite satisfactory, undivided existence.

A delicate balance can be maintained unless and until the container begins to move toward the threshold of a foundational shift. Then, as it were, all hell can break loose. The container, who may have been committed to the marriage but not fully grounded in and encompassed by it, begins to encounter all the complexities and issues inherent in a developmental shift. He or she begins to feel himself less understood and supported in his or her efforts to deal with the tectonic forces in his life and may move toward other sources of support.

In the face of these threatening changes, the natural reaction of the contained mate is to cling ever-more tenaciously to the status quo. "The more the contained clings," observes Jung, "the more the container feels shut out of the relationship. The contained pushes into it by her clinging, and the more she pushes, the less the container is able to respond." To use Jung's colorful metaphor, the container may start to "spy out the window," looking for other sources of support, understanding, and succor.

Both partners in the relationship have a special mission at this critical moment. For the contained, it is most important to be able to see this struggle—be it mild or mighty—as something going on *within* the partner and not as something intended to disrupt their world. They simply cannot see this as a confirmation of their insecurities or a threat to their well-being. Having promised to be there "in sickness and in health," it might be well to consider this a form of "holy sickness" that calls forth the virtues of patience and nurturance in the contained, not resentment and rebukes. The toothpaste is already out of the tube. To try and put it back in is just going to make an awful mess. (Besides, the contained's turn is likely still to come.)

For the spouse who is functioning as the container this time around, your acts of consciousness include an awareness that your situation grants you no special status, no moral or intellectual superiority, and that this person to whom you have committed yourself has a need for patience and understanding quite equal to your own. And if you should find yourself "spying out the window," Jung would advise you to "become conscious of the fact that [you are] seeking completion, seeking the contentedness and undividedness that have always been lacking." That is your own inner need, particularly in times of transition and disunity. If your inner need is not being met, that is not necessarily someone else's fault. Your spouse, in short, is not your enemy.

Which leads us to the third act of consciousness.

The Enemy Is Us

A friend and sometime colleague, Hannah, seemed for all the world to have a perfectly terrible marriage. During the years of our association, I heard one story after another about her husband's indiscretions, emotional cruelty, and lack of sensitivity to her needs. He was unsupportive of her desire for personal growth and development, demeaning of her spiritual urges, and openly hostile to her attempts to become a more rounded person. Or so she said.

Hannah was clearly in the throes of a second foundational shift, though it had been pushed to her late forties by child-rearing and career. She seemed on the cusp of important and significant changes in her life and relationships. If only she had the understanding and support of her husband, Dick …

But as I watched her journey unfold in the years I knew her, I saw something that genuinely surprised me. As the kids left the nest and she became more self-sufficient in her career, most of us expected that the next news we would hear was that Hannah was separating herself from an abusive, stultifying marriage.

That never happened, and for one simple reason: Dick was not the enemy. Whatever was or was not true about him as a husband, the fear, doubt, and inertia that kept Hannah from moving forward in her life lay within Hannah herself. Her *negative* projections onto her husband allowed her to set up a straw man whom she could blame for her own shortcomings. Life becomes immeasurably easier when all your problems can be blamed on someone else.

Hannah's case is a bit extreme and grew out of her own particular psychology and life experiences. It is also true that there are many marriages—sad things to behold—where one spouse holds an inordinate amount of power over the other and uses it to crush the life out of anything new that threatens to emerge. (As has often been said, it is power, not hate, that is the opposite of love.) But in most relationships, partnerships, and marriages, we are the enemies of our own growth.

We stand in our own way, content to cast the blame upon that person who was, after all, *supposed* to be all-understanding, all-forgiving, and all-loving.

So when a man awakens in the midst of a foundational shift to the realization that part of his life has gone unlived, that he has unrealized goals, that there are things he wants to be and do and experience and become, he'd best not start by blaming the woman in his life. If he has the courage to look at his situation consciously and objectively, he will find more often than not that those things could be accomplished within the context of his current relationship—that is, if he doesn't cling to a worn-out anima image that says his woman is responsible for making him whole and for making sure his unrealized expectations get met.

SOME SUGGESTIONS

We can be conscious of our own patterns of projection, of our roles as "container" and "contained," and of the inner enemy within us and still find ourselves faced with the most gnawing and consequential choice we will ever make in our lifetimes. No marriage remains unchanged in the wake of one of life's foundational shifts. This is particularly true of the second, midlife shift, even if the partners silently conspire to keep all surface appearances the same.

But what will be the outcome? Do the partners commit or submit to a working-through of the old relationship with some distinctly new terms and understandings? Do they buy their peace for the sake of stability? At what price? Do one or both partners decide to break away from the current relationship as their best hope of satisfaction in life, and have they sufficiently shed their illusions about themselves and the other so such a thing becomes possible?

As in the previous chapter on career choices, there are no silver-bullet answers. But here are some things to consider:

1. *See beyond the Projections.* The first thing to do is the most obvious, and yet often the most sorely neglected: talk, listen, talk some more, and if you have problems breaking through the barriers to honest conversation, get help learning how to talk and listen. Your projections and expectations of the other may have robbed you of your ability to truly know what is

going on inside him or her. Be curious and nonjudgmental as you seek to truly understand what makes the other person tick. As bizarre as it may seem, we are often more aware of the inner workings of our children, friends, and coworkers than we are of the person who sleeps next to us each night—precisely because those relationships are less subjected to the assumptions and expectations our projections produce. Taking nothing for granted, get to know what your partner most loves, fears, hopes for, values, and wishes to change.

2. *Access Others.* In addition to talking more openly with your partner than perhaps you ever have, bring other people into the process as well. The more questions and challenges you get from impartial observers, the more you can solidify your own thinking and see through your own illusions. But take care here—you may need to choose confidants who are objective professionals, or who have been through similar crises, or whom you respect for their particular wisdom and open-mindedness. Ironically, you may need to discount the advice of "friends" during this time. Remember that the people closest to you are likely to have their own projections about you, making objectivity more difficult for them. Close friends in particular may have a vested interest in seeing you maintain the status quo since it is less threatening to them.

3. *Take Your Share of the Responsibility.* All the talking, listening, exploring, and understanding in the world cannot change the fact that some marriages simply cannot contain and foster the growth and well-being of the individuals in it. It is a sad but inevitable truth that for some couples, the love potion can never morph into contented commitment. Worse yet, the love potion can turn into a kind of poison that stifles and subdues the God-given gifts and potentialities of one or both partners. But if you feel this to be your situation, you must be able to look yourself squarely in the face and answer these questions:
   • What changes would be necessary in the relationship for it to be healthier and more livable, and are those changes

possible? Notice I did not ask what changes your *partner* would need to make but what changes would be necessary in the character and quality of the *relationship*.

- How have I contributed to these issues, and what can I do about it? Note again that I am not asking how your partner is to blame. Laying problems at their feet is generally a way of excusing your own inaction. How are you contributing, and how can you change?

- And finally, the mother of all cautionary questions: Am I considering leaving the relationship because I want to bolt to *another* relationship that is more appealing? Am I leaving because I think that man or woman waiting in the wings for me would solve all my problems and bring me true happiness? If anything has been learned from this chapter concerning projection and romantic love, the dangers of that kind of thinking should be obvious. As weighty and consequential as marriage is (or for that matter any long-term relationship), it should stand or fall of its own merits and not as a result of the distant lure of a Prince Charming or a Fair Maiden. Otherwise our happily-ever-after could end up as "here we go again."

4. *Avoid Escapism.* Are you wanting to escape to a "new life"? Inevitably, a number of the couples my wife and I knew in our twenties and thirties went the way of separation and divorce. Nothing new there. But in a few instances, one or both of the partners would "fall in love" again, pull up roots, move to a new city, and systematically cut all ties with friends and coworkers who, just a few years earlier, had been their dearest friends.

"It is possible," says Robert Kegan, "that this phenomenon is a function of our inability to work out the anger and shame attendant on evolutionary development in the context of the relationship or environment that provoked it. It is possible that we turn to the new community and new relationships with a belief that 'here, only the new me will be known' and that these new others, in their not knowing, will help me leave my old self behind." I am not denying the need many people have for a "fresh start" after the end of a relationship, but there are two problems with this kind of escapism. The first, of course, is that our old self continues to tag along to our new relationships and communities unless we make the kinds of fundamental and lasting changes that *conscious choice* might allow. But the second problem Kegan points out is that serial relationships and communities come at a price. "Long-term relationships in life in a community of considerable duration may be essential if we are not to lose ourselves, if we are able to recollect ourselves. They may be essential to the human coherence of our lives." Escapism can be a fetching notion when facing life's difficulties and choices; but like a character in a Hemmingway novel, you may find that life on an anonymous island is not all it's cracked up to be.

5. *Focus on What Is.* How can you jump-start the process of reeling in your projections? How can you expose the negative projections that may be causing you to blame your partner for your own discontent? How can you spot the positive projections that may be making your newfound lover unrealistically attractive to you? Robert Johnson suggests that you sit down and write yourself a "what is" letter. Here are the rules: you can't talk about what once was, what might be, or what ought to be. Moreover, you need to avoid abstractions and stick to specifics. Statements such as, "I am miserable because my wife doesn't understand me" won't pass the test. You cannot blame or idealize or theorize— you have to stick with what is. Several years ago, a dear friend of mine was passionately and uncontrollably attracted to a woman with whom he worked. They were "in love." But as he agonized over his own what-is letter, an interesting pattern emerged. His relationship with this woman existed almost completely in the realm of idealization and fantasy. The more their day-to-day interactions comported to the demands of reality, the more mundane and even troublesome their relationship became. "It was like we existed in a kind of bubble," he later reflected. "When we could sneak off for a weekend together and could live inside that bubble, it was pure heaven. But the truth is she

didn't have a lot of interest in some other parts of my life that were important to me, like my kids, and I noticed that I was really reluctant to get involved with her family or friends. I just wanted to live in the bubble. But that wasn't reality." In time, when my friend had successfully pulled back his projections from his coworker, he embarked on another what-is letter with respect to his life with his current spouse. Stripped of projection and blame, "what is" wasn't so bad!

6. *Look Inside, Not Outside.* Finally, accept the fact that every choice we make (including a choice not to choose) is our own responsibility and is a response to forces at work within us, not outside us. In his provocative work *Control Theory* (he later changed the terminology to "choice theory"), William Glasser argues convincingly that at any given moment, all we do, think, or feel comes from our own inner attempts to satisfy certain basic drives. These drives include the need for a sense of belonging, for personal freedom, for fun, and for a sense of competence and power in our own lives. Nothing we do is caused by what happens outside of us but constitutes our best response at the time to these forces and needs within us. Seen in this way, it becomes awfully difficult to hold other people responsible for our own misery.

    In fact, Glasser gives four reasons why we might unconsciously choose to continue our own misery rather than make more effective choices: 1) to keep our anger under control; 2) to manipulate other people into helping us; 3) to excuse our unwillingness to do something more effective for ourselves; or 4) to gain power and control over another. If this is true—and my experience tells me it is—then it begs you to ask yourself four important questions. Simply put, they are:
    *   What do you want? What of your most basic needs are not being met to your satisfaction?
    *   What are you doing to get what you want?
    *   How is that working for you?
    *   If it is not working, what is the next thing you are going to do or try? And let's be clear: you are not allowed to throw

your hands up in despair. There is *always* something else to be done or tried.

These questions are simple but extremely powerful. You may need to sit with them for weeks or even months before you are clear on what you want, what you are doing to get it, whether that is working, and what else to do. But in time, it will rob you of the instinctive need to blame others and will lead you to a more thoughtful and less reflexive response to the issues of relationships, love, and marriage.

Mistakes

Last night, as I was sleeping,
I dreamt—marvelous error!—
That I had a beehive
Here inside my heart.
And the golden bees
Were making white combs
And sweet honey
From my old failures.

—Antonio Machado,
"Last Night As I Was Sleeping"
(trans. by Robert Bly)

If you bring forth what is in you, what you bring forth will save
you; if you do not bring forth what is within you, what you do
not bring forth will destroy you.—The Gospel of Thomas

"To ERR IS HUMAN." Of course, we know that. We are all perfectly and painfully aware that life cannot be lived without mistakes. Even the Christian admonition to "be ye perfect" (Matthew 5:48, King James Version) relies on a questionable translation of the Greek word *teleiosis*, which is better understood as "connoting something that is completed, matured, or having reached its ultimate goal," rather than something incapable of error. But that doesn't ease our regret—for the pain caused by leaving a relationship too soon or too late; for being blinded by our projections and blind to reality; for the career path not taken or the one taken at great cost.

While we are permitted our regrets (and those who profess to have none are a dangerous lot indeed), we should not try too hard to forget about our mistakes or to assign them to the recycle bin of our mind. In an important way, we can redeem them. In an even more important way, they may already have redeemed us.

LEARNING HOW TO DRIVE BY RUNNING INTO THINGS

I remember the first time my father let me drive the family car. I very self-assuredly backed out of the driveway and directly into the curb across the street. *Ka-whomp!* It was not the last curb (or mailbox or lamppost) that I would hit, but I did get better over time at mastering that particular task of adulthood. That is, until I started traveling extensively in those countries that drive on the "wrong" side of the road, where I raised curb butting to a veritable art form.

Driving, like many other things in life, is a self-regulating system. If we veer too far from the highway we'll encounter one of those teeth-jarring rumble strips. If we go too slowly, we'll hear about it from the horns of other motorists. If we go too fast, there will likely be a blue light somewhere along the way to remind us and even stop us. Hopefully in more of a metaphoric than literal sense, we learn how to drive by running into things. Mistakes are how we learn stuff.

With the thornier and less purely mechanical challenges of life, it can seem like it is necessary for us to cover the same ground, repeat the same patterns, and make pretty much the same mistakes over and over again. It can look and feel as if we are traveling in a circle. But on closer examination, the circle may be more of an upward spiral; with every turn around that bend we are up a little higher, have a little better perspective, and are able to see the pattern more clearly. In fact, the spiral is an excellent visual image of what personal growth looks like during a time of foundational shift. What appears to be a repetition is actually a deepening of experience and awareness, with consciousness of our own self-regulating systems as an ultimate goal. We can redeem our mistakes from the junk heap of our lives if we can come to see them as the necessary correctives that they were.

To quote Parker Palmer, the religious author and activist whose books on finding one's vocation in life are among the best ever written on the subject:

> I do not feel despondent about my mistakes ... though I grieve the pain they have sometimes caused others. Our lives are "experiments with truth" (to borrow the subtitle of Gandhi's autobiography), and in an experiment negative results are at least as important as successes. I have no idea how I would have learned the truth about myself and my calling without the mistakes I have made ...

In another sense, we might want to consider the possibility that it is our mistakes that are redeeming *us*. The more life I have behind me to examine, the more convinced I become that if left solely to my own ego and its will, I would have made a terrible mess of things. There were unexpected turns that were the furthest thing from what I consciously wanted to happen. There were shocks to the system that knocked me completely aback and turned me around. There were mistakes, and there were out-and-out blunders.

Yet I can look back now and see sense in the patchwork, an inner coherence that led me to the work I've done, the places I've been, and the people I have known and loved. If I had been scripting it, I would have screwed it up. So there has always been a belief—more accurately a knowing—that the script was being coauthored.

This is not a kind of fatalism that says it is all in the stars or the cards, and thus it is useless to concern ourselves with things like human initiative. You can call it the unconscious, or fate, or God—the words matter less than the objective reality. But there is a force capable of using our personal defeats for our greater good and may even engineer them.

Freud believed that our blunders sometimes burst forth from our own suppressed desires and conflicts. So the man whose job has become intolerable may make a huge error in calculating a bid, or a woman in a dead-end marriage may leave behind evidence of her infidelity. I have known multiple versions of similar situations to actually happen, and while in each case the error was unintended, the "victims" would later acknowledge that something within them seemed to be seeking rescue from their current situations.

As Joseph Campbell so eloquently put it in his *Hero with a Thousand Faces*: "[Blunders] are ripples on the surface of life, produced by unsuspected springs. And these may be very deep—as deep as the soul itself. The blunder may amount to the opening of a destiny … The familiar life horizon has been outgrown; the old concepts, ideals, and emotional patterns no longer fit; the time for the passing of a threshold is at hand."

Shortly before his death in 1961, Jung was asked by an interviewer about his idea of God. He replied, "To this day, God is the name by which I designate all things which cross my willful path violently and recklessly, all things which upset my subjective views, plans, and intentions and change the course of my life for better or worse."

If we can admit the possibility that at least some of life's most bitter pills were in fact the medicine designed to cure us, if we can see the redemptive power of our own mistakes, then we can still regret, but we can never despair.

Sarah Beeson

Not all mistakes are redeemable. My client Sarah Beeson was, to my mind, one of those tragedies. She was (and still is) a very bright, witty, and engaging manager with one of the current telecommunications giants. Sarah was blessed—gifted, really—with an exceptional ability to plan and implement complex projects. "The best damned project manager I'd seen in twenty years of this kind of work," said one peer.

Not surprisingly, Sarah's success and skills eventually resulted in a significant promotion to vice president in charge of quality and process improvement for a large segment of the corporation. No longer shepherding projects herself, she was called upon to provide leadership to a professional staff and to interface with senior executives whose divisions looked to Sarah's staff for advice and suggestions.

And that was when the trouble started. Busy executives wanted top-line, crisp communications from their process advisor. But over the years, Sarah had formed something of a love affair with details—absorbing them, sorting them, and moving them around like pieces on a game board. And most of all she liked *talking* about them—endlessly.

To listen to Sarah's explanation of a project was like reading *War and Peace* and wondering if you would ever get to the end. Higher-ups in the organization viscerally suffered through her presentations, which were overly long, convoluted, and repetitive. Simple questions were met with overly detailed answers. So proud was she of her store of information, and gleeful to impart it to others, that she would completely miss the cues that she was losing and often irritating her audience.

Moreover, Sarah prided herself on her quick wit and her independent-mindedness, which often migrated over into sarcasm and irreverence regardless of the level of the person to whom she was speaking. Those qualities had actually been an advantage early in her career (recall our discussion of the "Formula for Success" in our chapter on the second foundational shift) as she fought her way up the ladder of a male-dominated business. But times and protocols had changed. At one group dinner, where the visiting CEO of the company was present, she made a sarcastic remark so inappropriate that the CEO was personally offended and said as much to Sarah's direct supervisor the following day.

When the company called me in to work with Sarah, they told me she had already "run through" another executive coach. Yet I had no reason to be other than optimistic, given how clear her issues were and how bright she seemed to be. It took the better part of a year working together, but she was finally able to disabuse me of my optimism.

Yes, she did "get it" on an intellectual level. She saw how her communication style was viewed by senior management and made some cosmetic changes. She saw how her humor and iconoclasm were perceived by others and attempted to do more self-monitoring. But the truth is, the things she was being asked by others to change or tone down were far too linked to the ways in which she defined herself, and that self-definition was simply too precious to let go. She was in love with, betrothed to, the image she had created for herself, and to change in any way seemed somehow unfaithful.

In the end, she managed to convince herself that staying as she was wouldn't really impact her career. A year later, a forced lateral transfer would prove her wrong. She kept her title but was moved to a role where continued advancement was highly unlikely.

There is nothing wrong, mind you, with liking parts of yourself that do not fit with the prevailing corporate culture. In fact, in our chapter

"Choices I," we met another client of mine named Keith Hamilton who appropriately opted for authenticity over conformity and was the better for it. But Sarah's situation did not have that flavor. She felt to me like an immature and petulant child in a grownup body, fearful of "taking a new step, uttering a new word" (to borrow Dostoevsky's phrase), as if her constructed self-image could not abide a challenge to its supreme rule. Even if "witty," "unconventional," and "detail-oriented" had now translated into inappropriate, unprofessional, and obstructionist, it wasn't worth the candle to her to see that behavior in its true light.

Sarah Beeson made a career-derailing mistake because she was listening too intently to one of the Four Voices—first discussed in "Choices I"—which can keep us from making intelligent and life-giving choices. Sarah heard the voice of Vanity, and as long as it claimed her allegiance, she had no chance to redeem the mistakes she was making, much less be redeemed by them.

A DEVIL'S BARGAIN—THE "FOUR VOICES" REVISITED

So it is too with the voices of Obligation, Security, and "Reality." Any of the Four Voices can prompt us into making the one unpardonable sin, the one irredeemable error. They can lead us, like Sarah, to do nothing at all.

Though Gail Sheehy's best-selling book *Passages* is now somewhat dated in its treatment of gender roles, she correctly points out that men are somewhat more attuned to the voice of Obligation than are women. Despite the preponderance of two-income families in our current society, men are acculturated to believe that theirs is the role of primary breadwinner, even if they are not.

"If a man insists upon maintaining, or accepts without a whimper, the status quo of roles that says all economic burdens should be on his shoulders (and many do), then he must face up to the fact that there is no light at the end of his tunnel. He is locked in for good. The last breath he draws will be to say, 'The insurance is paid up, honey,' because he will be taking care of his wife even after he is dead." Obligation, to the extent that it drowns out more authentic voices and choices, can deaden us to everything else life has to offer—and to what we have to offer to the world.

I have always thought the term "conventional wisdom" to be something of an oxymoron. We think of wisdom as the kind of individual discernment, understanding and judgment that sets one apart from the commonplace and the trite. Yet to be "conventional" is just that—lacking in individuality, originality, or creativity. The voice of Security is the very mouthpiece of conventional wisdom. You know all the trite and time-worn admonitions: "Keep your head down and your nose clean," "Fly under the radar," and "Don't rock the boat." We opt for what Robert Quinn calls "the strategy of peace and pay."

As I write this, the United States is locked in the worst recession in seventy-five years. In such economic circumstances, it may well be that wisdom is aligned with convention in suggesting that the voice of Security be carefully heeded. With unemployment at double digits in some parts of our country, this may not be the best time for making risky personal or economic choices. But by the time these words come to print, that situation will likely have improved, and the strategy of peace and pay will again come at a cost.

Quinn is blunt in his assessment of that cost: "When people do this, they are coping with slow death by choosing slow death. Their resignation traps them in a vicious cycle from which escape is difficult. They shake their heads and condemn the organization, rightly noting that the organization is dying and wrongly assuming that they are not. The peace-and-pay strategy is a form of mental illness. Actively choosing peace and pay means deliberately joining the legions of the walking dead." Once again, we may think that we are actively choosing for things to remain the same. But in the longer run, they never do.

Finally, we all know people who live their lives almost completely by the principle of delayed gratification—a fine principle, mind you, if it is not applied to your entire life. "Just fifteen more years until retirement, and I'm out of this egg-sucking job." "As soon as the mortgage is paid up, then we can really start to live." "When the kids are finally independent, then I can decide whether staying in this marriage is the right thing to do." Yes, there are legitimate concerns inherent in these statements about Obligation (I should), Security (I dare not), and Vanity (How would this look?). But beneath them all is the conviction that it's just not "Realistic" to do anything else. Never mind that many others make different choices about their relationships and it turns out fine;

or that there are people who are never fortunate enough to get out of debt during their lifetimes but still manage to save for what makes them happy; or that people all over the world (or in times past) have never even heard of a pension or a 401K.

For all too many people, being "Realistic" means you that get the best income-potential education you can, snag the highest-paying job you can, sock away as much money as you can while buying as much stuff as you can, and then when the kids are gone and the mortgage is paid and some magic age or bank balance is achieved, you can *finally* do the things you always wanted to do. Such is, in any event, the conventional wisdom.

But there are two problems with this "Realistic" worldview, one obvious and one not as much. The first, of course, is that "stuff happens." Things rarely turn out as you script them. People die. Stock markets crash. There's a note on the kitchen table and the closet is empty. Depending on your religious tradition, we're only assured of one lifetime on this earth. What you are living right now is not a dress rehearsal for some future gala production. It's the real deal. Your choices need to reflect that.

But second, we would do well to remember a basic tenet of high school geometry. Picture two lines diverging from a central point—the old fork in the road. As the distance from the point of divergence lengthens, the two lines themselves grow farther and farther apart. And so it is with the paths you choose for your own life. You might think the road you have chosen (e.g., "just fifteen more years to retirement") is running nicely parallel to the life you would prefer—that you could hop across that divide at any moment and find yourself truly happy.

But it doesn't work that way. The angle of divergence, with each passing month and year, puts you further and further away from the life you dream about and makes it ever more inaccessible to you. You change. The world around you changes. You become more of what you pretend to be and move ever further from what you could have been. It's a bit like a passenger jet that takes off from New York headed for Europe. A variance in the flight plan of just a few degrees and it will end up in Africa instead—with not enough fuel to correct the mistake.

That is why this kind of "Realism" is a devil's bargain. You choose the path you are on because you wish to be sensible, safe, and secure.

But you can lose your very soul, or, if you prefer more secular language, the essence of who you really are and the promise of who you could be. "We may think there is a sure road," said Jung, "But that would be the road of death. Then nothing happens any longer—at any rate, not the right things. Anyone who takes the sure road is as good as dead."

It is this quote from Jung that may help us to decipher the baffling words attributable to Jesus in the Gospel of Thomas, found among the Dead Sea Scrolls in 1947 (see the opening quotes of this chapter). To bring forth that which is inside you requires that you put the Four Voices in their proper place—and may sometimes require that you eschew them altogether. If taking the sure road means failing to live your true life, you may paradoxically have put yourself in great peril. Life has a force of its own apart from our consciousness and, if denied, will act against us as if it were some external force.

"Then the conflict hits one from the outside rather than from the inside," psychologist Edward Edinger observes. In that case, our misfortunes are felt as "bad luck," or "the breaks," or karma, or Fate. At best, it can leave us in our later years unfulfilled, bitter, and ill. At worst, as Jesus says, it can destroy us.

Make Your Experiment

This may displease some of my fundamentalist Christian friends, but I have never read the Gospels as telling me that Jesus was perfect. Indeed, some of the texts of the Apocrypha and other early writings excluded from the Christian New Testament show a Jesus who was anything but perfect. There were harsh emotions. There was error. There were baffling and sometimes contradictory statements. There was temptation. There was doubt.

But this is certain: at some point in his life on Earth, he became clear about who he was and why he was here. He followed that vision thereafter with all of his human will and against all of the conventions of his time, even unto death. It is that central fact that gives him the status of prophet or saint in each of the world's major religions, even if they do not accept the Christian assertion of his divinity.

Life asks no less of us, though the challenge is unique and inimitable for each individual. Borrowing from the Jewish proverb, I do not so much fear that God will ask of me, "Why were you not Jesus?" but I would greatly dread the question, "Why were you not Michael?" As the

Jewish author Lawrence Jaffe put it, "We must all do just what Christ did. We must make our experiment. We must make mistakes. We must live out our own vision of life. And there will be error. If you avoid error, you do not live."

To make our experiment is to see our mistakes as redeemable, and our lives as capable of being redeemed by them. It is the ability to endure the incomprehensible—in a job loss or a failed relationship or an illness—knowing that the central character in the drama plays on, perhaps one day to see how the pieces snugly fit together. To quote once more from Parker Palmer:

> In retrospect, I can see in my own life what I could not see at the time—how the job I lost helped me to find work I needed to do, how the "road closed" sign turned me toward terrain I needed to travel, how losses that felt irredeemable forced me to discern meanings I needed to know. On the surface, it seemed that life was lessening, but silently and lavishly the seeds of new live were always being sown.

Life has its own motive force, for those who choose to step into its flow. And mistakes are not just unavoidable—they are essential to a life well-lived.

Propellers and Sandbars

*I call a man awake who knows in his conscious reason his innermost
unreasonable forces, drives, and weaknesses and knows how to deal
with them. For you to learn about yourself is the potential reason
for your having met me. You've forgotten your childhood; it cries
for you from the depths of your soul. It will make you suffer until
you heed it.*—Herman Hesse, *Narcissus and Goldmund*

*It is from need and distress that new forms of life take their
rise, and not from mere wishes or from the requirements of our
ideals.*—Carl Jung, *Modern Man in Search of a Soul*

IN THE VAST SHALLOWS of the Congo River, often two miles across,
danger takes an unexpected form. Our pilot, Andre, knows the hazards
all too well, as well as he seems to know every eddy and sandbar of this
muddy blackness that drains the world's second-largest river basin. We
are in a hewn dugout, the same kind of vessel that has traversed the
Congo for thousands of years—only now we have the luxury of a small
outboard motor on the stern.

Andre propels us upriver, changing courses as often as a viper in
tall grass. But then, in response to something that seems more felt than
seen, he slows the dugout to coasting speed and lifts the propeller out
of the water completely. Sure enough, dimly visible only when we are
directly above it, a sandbar passes beneath us. The dugout's smooth
bottom slides harmlessly across it, and we are off again.

In lilting French, Andre explains why he must be so careful. Lose the propeller, he says, and we are at the complete mercy of the currents. If we are lucky, we will merely end up on the impoverished shores of Brazzaville on the north side of the river or in the war-ravaged city of Kinshasa to the south. If we are not so lucky, we'll drift into the crushing rapids ten kilometers to the west of here.

In the journey that is our lives, there are times for forward movement, and one can hardly argue that a propeller isn't superior to a paddle when making one's way upstream. There are also times to coast—to feel our way along with an intense awareness of our situation and surroundings. But there are also sandbars out there. They don't just delay us; they can rob us of our motive force, suck us dry of energy, or leave us dangerously adrift.

Where is Andre when we need him?

EGO AS SANDBAR

"The fault," said the Bard, "is not in our stars / But in ourselves …" And it is there that one of life's most dangerous sandbars lies.

The ego is the instrument of our consciousness, our window to the world. For a child who is deprived through trauma or neglect of an opportunity to build a strong ego identity, the result is almost always extreme psychological difficulties later in life. When the ego of an adolescent or young adult is crushed by outer circumstance, the result is tragic indeed. But for almost all of us, that is not the problem. Throughout the process of growing up, we are building our egos brick by brick, until we have constructed something that both defines us to the world and protects us from it. We polish it, preen it, expand it, parade it—but most of all, we *protect* it.

John A. Sanford, who has the twin vocations of Episcopal priest and Jungian analyst, puts it succinctly in many of his lectures: "The ego is a great cheat." It will deflect criticism by placing the blame elsewhere. It will see its position as right and just even in the face of overwhelming logic. When faced with abject failure, it may borrow a line from the old song and "pick yourself up, dust yourself off, start all over again," oblivious to the fact that the failure may have been a strong message to go in a different direction. Should a successful assault or outright defeat for the ego force a reevaluation, the results are likely to be temporary and minor.

This truth prompted Fritz Kunkel (who was John Sanford's mentor) to say, "In [this] case we simply have a change at the periphery of one's life and not at the center. It is the evasive way of improving one's habits without actually correcting the mistake in the ego."

Almost all of us are egocentric. Technically, that merely means our egos occupy the central place in our personal universe. Just ask someone renown for their altruism whether part of their motivation is the way it makes *them* feel about themselves, and see whether you get the smile of a Mother Theresa or the snarl of a defensive ego. Or listen to (or read) the prayers of the truly pious and see how often they seek forgiveness for their daily sins of selfishness.

The problem, of course, is that while the ego tries very hard to defend itself against challenge and change, that is precisely what life's transitions will foist upon us. Sarah Beeson's story in the preceding chapter is but one example of the danger of letting our egos—our carefully constructed self-concepts—stand in the way of life's forward flow. As Jung observed, "The only thing that moves nature is causal necessity, and that goes for human nature too. Without necessity nothing budges, the human personality least of all. It is tremendously conservative, not to say torpid. Only acute necessity is able to rouse it."

In the first transitional shift, that "necessity" may consist of finding one's own way in the world free from childhood ties and illusions. In the second shift, it may come in the realization that the ego's formula for success has now become a recipe for failure. In the third, a sense of narrowing time horizons may necessitate a broadening of our perspective—"business as usual" won't cut it anymore.

And lest the reader think advancing age and accumulated life experience can provide protection against the sandbar of egocentricity, consider the story of a man named David.

By the time he was in his fifties, David had come to a place in his life that most would find enviable. He held a comfortable teaching position, had raised three fine children to adulthood, had a broad circle of friends, and was possessed of a marriage that had lasted for decades.

But the subterranean forces of the third foundational shift were at work in David—and he was not handling them well.

He was feeling the onset of his limitations far more than he was exploring his gifts. As long walks replaced his daily trips to the gym, and it became apparent that further advancement in his academic career was unlikely, David began to succumb to the one sin our egos are most prone to commit during such times: instead of exploring and embracing the tensions between his limitations and his uniqueness, David decided he was, in a word, "special."

His friends noticed his increasingly effete affectations and his sudden snobbery about gourmet fare, but they took it all in stride. His colleagues merely rolled their eyes as his graying hair fell to ponytail length but murmured as his opinions on the subjects of the day became more strident and self-righteous. And his wife of thirty years was caught completely off guard when he announced that the marriage no longer served any useful purpose for him and took up with a waitress at a local deli (half his age, of course, in keeping with his "specialness"). Even now, David's former wife struggles to make sense of what happened: "He went from being a very genuine and sincere person to being something of a parody of himself. It's like, being known as a 'character' became more important than being known as Dave."

Fueled by adoring students who see him as a 1960s throwback, and enabled by administrators who love to parade him as a symbol of faculty diversity, David has found his niche. And here's betting that he is all too comfortable with it—at least for now—to suspect that it is also a sandbar.

In T. S. Eliot's play *The Cocktail Party*, the artful psychologist Sir Henry Harcourt-Reilly is confronting the play's central character, Edward, who seems obsessed with seeing his case as "very unusual" and himself as quite special. Says Reilly:

> I could make you feel important,
> And you would imagine it a marvelous cure;
> And you would go on, doing such amount of mischief
> As lay within your power—until you came to grief.
> Half of the harm that is done in this world
> Is due to people who want to feel important.

They don't mean to do harm—but the harm does not interest them.
Or they do not see it, or they justify it
Because they are absorbed in the endless struggle
To think well of themselves.

SUFFERING

Those in the throes of a foundational shift will describe a variety of negative emotions that, at least at times, seem to beset and even paralyze them: anxiety, despair, depression, a sense of loss, grief, doubt, fear. It could hardly be otherwise. The new life that is bubbling up from within you is meeting the encrusted mass that is your current self-image and way of life. Small wonder that there is a sense of anxiety, for something within you is indeed being "de-pressed."

Small wonder, too, that we will continue to live out of our old patterns—and may even redouble our efforts—in order to keep that inner shift at bay. But at some point a critical mass is reached, the molten springs find their way to the surface, and something the psychologists call a decompensation occurs. We repeat our patterns, but their old efficacy is gone. No parent, no lover, no bottle of vodka can rescue us. What we believed to be our center cannot hold. We suffer.

But there is an absolute world of difference between transitional suffering that is understood and accepted as part of the process and that which is unconscious, ignored, or fought against. In this case, ignorance is not bliss; ignorance is unnecessarily painful.

To Jung, "A neurosis must be understood, ultimately, as the suffering of a soul which has not discovered its meaning." I have always understood that quote to mean that while suffering is an inevitable part of our humanity, it loses its power to make us mentally ill when we understand what it means and why it is there. For a person who is undergoing one of life's foundational shifts, that meaning and purpose is both clear and perfectly understandable. We are in the midst of change, both inwardly and outwardly. What was comfortable, important, or even inviolate to us may be called upon to change along with us. There is grief for what seems to have been lost, anxiety over a future not yet fully revealed, and perhaps confusion over choices yet to be made. It can be a dark and foreboding time. But unlike the caterpillar that spins its cocoon and starts its metamorphosis out of biological necessity, we have the capacity to understand that this is part of life's flow and choose to enter into it.

"This is the salvation through self-despair," William James wrote. "To get to it, a critical point must usually be passed, a corner turned within one. Something must give way, a native hardness must break down and liquefy."

I am reminded that one of the original meanings of the verb "to suffer" in our language was simply to *allow*—as when Jesus said, "Suffer the little children to come unto me" (Matthew 19:14, KJV). This is what Robert Johnson calls "creative suffering," which means to accept and allow what is going on in your life, knowing that it is part and parcel of a process that leads to *greater* life. It means a cessation of hostilities against the natural flow of your life so that the process may lead you to a new plateau. "Allowed" in this way, Johnson says, "Suffering may shake us out of the stupor of a provisional life, shatter our illusions of control, throw over naïve and immature attitudes, and force us to consciously consider our relationships with other people and with God."

It is here that we would do well to consider the notion of "sacrifice" in its original religious sense. Derived from the Latin root *sacrificium* ("to make holy"), to sacrifice means to give up something of value in order to obtain something of inestimably greater value. It seems to be a part of the life of every prophet and saint of all the world's great religions.

But it should be part of our own life's story as well. To give up the sense of familiarity and security that precedes each of life's transitions (what we called embeddedness in the introduction) is a sacrificial act. It is literally withdrawing the energy that has been invested in one stage of life and, over time, reinvesting it in a new and higher stage. It is giving up who you thought you were—and maybe wish you could have remained—for who you were meant to become. Perhaps that is one of the reasons why the story of Jesus' sacrifice, death, and resurrection is so compelling to us.

VULNERABILITY

That which is newly born is most vulnerable. Such is nature's law. That is never more evident than when we are going through a major shift in our lives. Mike King, whom we met in met in our chapters on "choices," recounts his experience during midlife this way:

> Here I was at my peak, both mentally and physically. I had put everything into this job and into what I had thought was going to be my lifelong career. I now understand what started to happen to me, but it sure was confusing at the time: not the same feelings about my job, not the same feelings about my marriage. I wanted to spend more time alone. I began wondering if I really wanted my boss's job after all.
>
> And then it started—on two fronts really. People at work started to ask, "What's wrong with Mike?" "Has he lost his edge?" "I wouldn't want to be him come next budget cycle." And it got to be just as bad at home—not so much the questions but the disapproving or disdainful looks I'd get when I mentioned some new book I was reading, or something I was thinking about, or when I'd mention maybe seeing a therapist.
>
> I felt pretty isolated at home and downright exposed at work.

Many of my clients report similar experiences as they move their way through a foundational shift. As discussed in the chapter "Choices II", the people closest to us may have a vested interest in our remaining as we are and may well feel threatened by the changes they perceive. At work, where power all too often trumps compassion, and competitiveness outweighs understanding, our changes may be seen as weakness—and an opportunity to pounce.

Changing course is not likely the answer, for another sandbar may await you. Stall, and you are headed for those crushing rapids below. These times call for a wary eye and the wise guidance of your own "Andre the pilot." Being forewarned is being forearmed.

THE FORCE OF UNLIVED LIFE

Fortunately, it is not all hidden sandbars along the way of life's transitions. We also can find hidden propellants in the process—sometimes in the most unlikely places.

Take, for example, the young man who though he had left his adolescent love of sports back home when he went off to college, only to find that same love of competition, challenge, and camaraderie right back at the surface when he achieved his first management role. Or the girl for whom piano lessons were a waste of good "hang time" with her buddies, but as a woman now finds herself drawn to creative expressions of all kinds. Or the guy in his fifties who always enjoyed being called "a man's man" but now gets his greatest satisfaction out of nurturing his grandkids and mentoring his younger employees. As Jung put it, "Many—far too many—aspects of life which should also have been experienced lie in the lumber-room among dusty memories; but sometimes, too, they are glowing coals under grey ashes."

This is the force of unlived life. In the process of growing up and becoming individuals, we inevitably make distinctions between what we *are* and what we *are not*. We cannot be everything, so we become split. But the trick here is that those parts of ourselves we shave off and banish to the lumber-room do not go away—they merely fall into our unconscious.

Jung defined this mysterious thing which psychologists call "the unconscious" in this way:

> Everything of which I know, but of which I am not at the moment thinking; everything of which I was once conscious but have now forgotten; everything perceived by my senses, but not noted by my conscious mind; everything which, involuntarily and without paying attention to it, I feel, think, remember, want, and do; all the future things that are taking shape in me and will sometime come to consciousness: all this is the content of the unconscious.

Literally every choice we make, course we set, and path we forsake has an unlived opposite that dwells in our unconscious. And it is as if that force were simply biding its time, storing its energy, so as to burst forth as a propellant in times of transition and change. That can be an extremely unsettling occurrence, but it can also be a saving grace, since we may desperately need that energy when we are stuck and floundering.

Not surprisingly, the emergence of that energy will often show itself in our dreams. Most people, I find, pay no attention to those nightly occurrences, if for no other reason than dreams are so difficult to understand. They speak in an abstract, symbolic language and often have the quality of a myth or fairy tale. Thus it is often only with wise guidance or extensive study that we can divine what a dream is really saying to us. For most of us in this consciously oriented, here-and-now world, that just doesn't seem worth the trouble.

But one of the most important roles our unconscious plays in our personal development is to compensate for the one-sidedness of our conscious views. If the conscious ego thinks—or wishfully believes—that the status quo is just fine and the seismic rumblings deep within us are just some form of mental indigestion, our dreams will be the first to let us know that the issue is more serious. Typical dreams at such a time include one's house being flooded, or an unusually large wave about to break over us. Perhaps the toilet is backing up or the place where we are standing is being undermined. Maybe it is snowing inside our house, or heavy weather is approaching on the horizon. Since water is a universal symbol for the unconscious, our dreams during transitional periods will often portray rivers, oceans, and malevolent weather as threatening or even terrifying forces.

Our dreams are not trying to frighten us—at other points in our lives water may symbolize nourishment, calm, or even spirituality. It is the ego's own frightened reaction to coming change that is the point of the dream.

The first part of our unlived life we are likely to encounter is what Jung calls our "shadow." This is usually a hallmark of the second, midlife foundational shift, but it can occur earlier, especially if the shadow is large enough and is suppressed for too long.

When I first met Cynthia, she was a very bright college student in her early twenties, seemingly mature beyond her years. She showed relatively less interest in dating than her peers, often instead burning the midnight oil in the campus study rooms. She dressed conservatively—some might say severely—and bore the reputation of being something of a prude. While any professor would consider her the ideal student, something was amiss.

I subsequently learned that, at a way too-early age, she had experienced a couple of limited but frightening sexual encounters.

Unable to deal consciously with what had happened, she let everything associated with those memories—including her own sexuality—fall into the unconscious. No wonder, then, that at the outset of her first foundational shift she had two important dreams back to back:

> In the first dream, I have lost my pocketbook. I think it has fallen into a well near my home, but it's too deep and I can't get to it. I'm panicking because all my stuff is in there—IDs, credit cards, pictures. I'm actually a lot more frantic than I would have been in real life—like some exaggerated reaction.

> In the second dream I turn on the overhead light in my bedroom. Thousands of cockroaches suddenly pour out of the light fixture and go everywhere. I am completely terrified of even one cockroach, but hundreds of them is the worst possible nightmare. I woke up terrified.

Cynthia was about to learn one of the axioms of unlived life: the more thoroughly we try to banish the more unpleasant or unwanted parts of ourselves into the shadow lands of the unconscious, the more strongly they will announce themselves upon their return. Cynthia was about to lose her "ID," her sense of who she was, and the false coherence she had constructed for the story of her life to date. When "illumination" came in the form of the overhead light (and yes, the dream chose a particular room of the house in order to make its point), the frightening memories and contents of the unconscious would have to be dealt with. They would not go away by just turning the light back off.

Like Cynthia, we tend to associate our shadow with things evil and worthy of banishment; like a bug to be exterminated. But there is much energy and potential in the neglected aspects of ourselves that can give our lives much more creativity and originality. It makes us more human, more accepting of others, more variegated, more interesting. People who suppress their "shadow side" are notoriously bland and uninteresting—but worse, they have the nasty habit of projecting their shadow onto people and groups they don't like. Moreover, when not consciously acknowledged, the shadow can erupt in ways that are embarrassing, inappropriate, or destructive. Witness the peccadilloes of so many of our public figures who purport to be the standard bearers for righteousness.

As James Hollis observes, "The shadow … represents our creativity, which abandoned, locks us into ennui and enervation. It embodies our spontaneity, which suppressed, routinizes, and stultifies our lives. It represents a life force greater than our conscious personality has yet utilized, and its blocking leads to diminished vitality."

As life stories go, Cynthia's has a very happy ending. The energy released from recognizing and dealing with her unlived life provided the accelerant that took her far as she navigated her first foundational shift. Now in her forties, she has used her native intelligence to obtain an MBA from a top-tier program, and she has achieved an uncommon degree of creativity as a corporate strategist. Most importantly, she and her husband have three terrific children, and she enjoys the kind of family life that might have eluded her if the *status quo ante* had prevailed.

While gender roles are less prescribed in our culture than they were in centuries past (and as the father of two daughters, I am pleased about that), the truth is that men and women remain wonderfully different genetically, physiologically, and emotionally. As an outgrowth of that, part of the unlived life of any man or woman will be the contrasexual tendencies (the personality traits most people repress because they are characteristic of the opposite sex) they shed, consciously or not, during the early stages of their lives. For example, a typical fifteen-year-old boy will be much more attuned to issues of physical power and assertiveness than his female counterpart, who will typically be relatively more interested in building caring relationships. By the time they reach adulthood, both will be ripe for the emergence of their contrasexual side.

Again, this is often most noticeable in midlife but can be seen peeking through in any of life's foundational shifts. James Simonton, whom we met in our chapter on the second foundational shift, freely admits he played a very masculine game of "seek and destroy" when he was the bank's turnaround specialist in Africa—rationally and dispassionately assessing a situation, dismembering the nonperforming assets (including people) as required, and leaving the pieces for someone else to deal with. It was only in midlife when that formula for success would no longer work for growing and sustaining a team that he had to (re)discover what it was like to be caring, nurturing, and enabling—and enjoy it. Taylor Gattis, whom we met in our first chapter, had to discover more of her masculine energy in asserting her selfhood and blazing her own path.

Robert Kaplan, in his decades of coaching corporate executives, has seen this phenomenon countless times:

> For male executives, [this shift] often means a move in the direction of the "feminine," embracing a reduction (even if modest) in their investment in work and an increase in their investment in personal relationships. For men to make this shift at midlife is to redefine themselves as being less thoroughly wrapped up in the quest for mastery, power, and rationality and more concerned with cultivating close, mutual, emotionally expressive relationships.

Seeing a woman give place to the masculinity within her or a man give voice to his femininity is one of the most satisfying things an executive coach (or parent, teacher, friend, or spouse) can witness. If done in appropriate measure, it can lead to a rounding out of personality and an immeasurable boost to our growth. But men and women are fundamentally different, and each can have, as it were, too much of a good thing. A women dominated by her masculine side is at best an "imitation man" (there are less complimentary descriptions in common parlance). A man under the control of his feminine side will be moody, petulant, and often irrational in his thought processes.

As Robert Johnson puts it, "Like fire, our contrasexual capacities make a wonderful servant but a terrible master." But as servants, these long-neglected parts of our personalities can be powerful propellers indeed.

But the most potent form of unlived life is also the most ancient within us. It predates the slow accumulation of our shadow side and the donning of our sex roles. It goes at least back to our early childhood, and if you believe in James Hillman's "acorn" theory, further back than that. In our chapter on the third foundational shift we described this inner force as The Dream—our earliest fantasies about how our unique combinations of loves and talents might play themselves out in the world. Yes, The Dream gets modified, and "real-ized," and sometimes lost altogether. But it is the "glowing coal under grey ashes" that can flame again during life's transitions. In fact, defying the natural order of things, those coals may burn hotter and flash more powerfully the longer they are neglected.

To illustrate, I'll finish a story I began earlier. A young Michael Thompson, galvanized by the black and white TV images of handsome attorneys in courtrooms where justice always prevailed, tried to find in the law an answer to his Dream's central command: "I want to help people do what they can't do for themselves."

The Dream took some direct hits early on. Law school taught me that my well-developed feeling side wasn't going to win me many arguments against my thinking-type classmates. Law practice, despite the outward decorum and gentility, was much more contentious than conciliatory—the reverse of my own nature. Worse yet, the practice of law was becoming, especially in the larger cities, more like a business and less like my idea of a profession. The Dream had to be "real-ized" if it was going to survive at all.

But survive it did. As I write this at the outset of my sixty-third year, I can see with clarity the times—sometimes long spans of it—when The Dream "lay in the lumber-room among dusty memories." But with every major shift and in every major decision, I can see how it made its voice heard and its insistence known. I could see it at work in the decision to move from private law practice into the corporate arena, where the contentiousness would not feel so unrelenting. I could see it flare up in the move toward teaching, where the university would not only allow me to touch individual lives but to broaden my interdisciplinary base into the realms of psychology, counseling, and leadership theory. And when the time came to move out of the relative shelter of the university setting, The Dream pointed me unerringly toward taking this strange admixture of learning and experiences into corporate coaching, counseling, and human development. I was, to the best of my abilities, helping people accomplish what they might not have accomplished without a little help.

But The Dream had at least one more twisty turn in store for me. I had long had a sneaking suspicion it might. When the economic meltdown of 2008 came, my business suffered like everyone else's. It seemed like all of my clients were either cutting back on the kinds of services I provided or, worse, were in bankruptcy. I had a choice: I could either plug away and await better days, or I could try something completely different. Not new, mind you, but different.

Those fuzzy 1950s images of courtroom victories were long gone, but many aspects of the original Dream were, if one were to brush away the ashes, alive and glowing—a genuine passion for helping others, a strong legal background, good counseling skills, and a knack for finding the compromise solution to thorny problems. All I needed was a way and place to apply them.

Today I still do some executive coaching and consulting work. But an equal joy comes in working "of counsel" with a rural, small-town law firm. My clients are primarily individuals and small-business owners with real-life and often thorny problems they could use a little help solving. I also mediate complex cases for our court system, trying to find workable solutions. Everything I ever learned, and every experience I ever had, gets a workout every single day. And it all feels much more like a profession than a business.

Given room, The Dream will out.

MEANINGFUL COINCIDENCES

We think of a "coincidence" as a confluence of events that is difficult to logically explain. Two American friends separately traveling abroad meet on the same street in Paris. Two American presidents die on July Fourth of the same year. The potential game-winning field goal sails "wide right" for a second consecutive season.

We find coincidences interesting, but we are endlessly looking for ways to rationally explain them. Maybe it was just random chance—think of all those millions of Americans who traveled to Europe who *didn't* run into each other. Perhaps there was causation involved, but it was just difficult to see—like the apprehensiveness of the kicker. In any event, we feel a lot safer if we can point to a rational reason for the confluence of those outer events.

But when an *inner* event connects with an outer event in an obvious way, it's a tougher sell to explain it away. It doesn't feel random at all. In fact, unless you insist upon trying to ignore it, there feels like there must have been some *meaning* associated with what just happened. Examples abound in everyone's life if we dare look for them. Perhaps you dream of a distant someone for whom you care and awake to find a message from them in your e-mail. Perhaps you are gripped by a mood of despair but find yourself stripped of your despondency by a brilliantly colored butterfly that seems to come from nowhere. A favorite and personal example of my own would include the fact that when I was making the career shift I described earlier in this chapter, I mistakenly hit the wrong key on my computer, revealing all the e-mails that had been captured by my spam filter. There, most recent among them, was an invitation to become involved in a project that directly led to the work I am doing now.

Jung referred to this confluence of inner and outer events as "synchronicity"—when something cannot be explained away by physical causality or understood as random chance. The only way it makes sense to the person experiencing it is in the way the inner and outer events seem linked together through some sort of surreptitious *meaning*. It has a *purpose* to it.

And that is scary because it forces us to acknowledge that the mental and physical worlds are not completely and neatly separate, that there is an almost playful interaction between the unconscious and the universe, and that ultimately, neither we nor random chaos are in full control.

And those realizations are never more important than during our experience of the foundational shifts. I do not know if we are more needful of life's synchronicities during those turbulent times or merely more aware of them. It hardly matters. The saving graces of synchronicity can help us preserve our sanity and stay our course. It may be a book that falls into your hands or a new acquaintance that changes everything. It could be a defeat that is transmuted into a new direction, even the illness that robs us of one faculty but sharpens the one more needed for this stage of the journey. It is the countless "slender threads," as Robert Johnson calls them, which at the critical junctures of our lives help guide and shape us and create our own unique tapestry.

That is, if we can put aside our search for safely rational explanations. Says Johnson:

I think the slender threads are continually present, it is just our ability to accept them that varies. It may be impossible for us to realize this because it would result in our seeing meaning everywhere and in all things. This is the perspective of the saint, but for most of us it is unbearable. It is probably true that we live in a universe with more meaning in it than we can comprehend or even tolerate. Life is not meaningless; it is overflowing with meaning, pattern, and connections.

A STILL, SMALL VOICE

Even great Hebrew prophets can stand a little help now and again. In the ninth-century BCE, Elijah was in pretty desperate straights. Many of his countrymen had turned away from the God of Abraham and were worshiping some dude named Baal. All of his fellow prophets had been killed, and he was on the run from the evil Jezebel and her henchmen. The best outcome he could hope for was to escape with his life.

But in one of the most poetic passages of the Judeo-Christian bible, we learn how Elijah went from the brink of despair, wishing for his own death, to the beginning of a new and unforeseeably heroic chapter in his life: "And behold, the Lord passed by, and a great and strong wind tore into the mountains and broke the rocks in pieces before the Lord, but the Lord was not in the wind; and after the wind an earthquake, but the Lord was not in the earthquake; and after the earthquake a fire, but the Lord was not in the fire; and after the fire a still small voice" (1 Kings 19:11–12).

When we are surrounded by the tumult of one of life's great shifts, we want the solutions to announce themselves just as nosily. Out of the cacophony of the winds and earthquakes and fires that seem to assail and threaten us, we would wish for a booming voice to rise above the racket and tell us what to do.

It is rarely thus. As Elijah was to understand, it was only by being attentive to that "still, small voice" that he would learn of his new direction and of the very next baby steps that needed to be taken in order to pursue his destiny. In my book *The Congruent Life*, I talked about the various ways we can train ourselves to hear that voice. Our intuitions, hunches, forebodings, and unexplained enthusiasms are not mere belches from the pit of our unconscious but can often be a deft signal of a path to be taken or a direction to be avoided. As I discussed in that earlier work, the disciplines of meditation, silence, and centering prayer in all of the world's religious traditions are meant to make one more open and discerning of those signals. But sometimes, too, that voice can be downright direct, as it was with Elijah.

In *The Congruent Life* I recount the story of a turning point in my own life—what I now call the first foundational shift. I was in my early thirties, with a responsible position as corporate counsel to a large financial institution but with an occasionally nagging sense that something was amiss. Amid all the trappings of "success," I often wondered if I was doing the right things for the right reasons in my life. I remember, in a way that three intervening decades cannot dim, driving down an interstate highway in my shiny company car, when a voice somewhere deep within me "said," in a way as real as if I had heard it with my ears: *You do not have to live like this!*

At first I paid the words no attention—the usual fate of most such messages. But the more they sank in, the more they seemed to speak to what I was deeply feeling but was unable to admit: I *wasn't* living life in a way that made me happy; I *wasn't* doing what I was best suited to do or doing it for the right reasons; I *wasn't*, to use Joseph Campbell's evocative line, "following my bliss"; and it *didn't* have to remain that way. Within a year I had a plan for transitioning out of that career situation and on to the next challenge of my life.

When such unconscious incursions take place during sleep we call them dreams. In fact, the various writers of the Judeo-Christian Bible seem to make no distinction between dreams, waking visions, and "night visions." Many of these nightly visitations reflect personal or archetypal contents that may be useful in therapy, but have little apparent connection to the great undercurrents in our lives. Others seem to have a sort of teleological quality to them, as if they are pulling us toward some future way of being. And during the shift points in our lives, our dreams can often be particularly vivid, plenteous, and insistent.

As dreams seem to delight in exaggerating our current situation in order to make us come to grips with it, they can be invaluable in providing a sort of "you are here" mark on life's highway map, even if they (maddeningly) do not always reveal a specific path forward. So one in a seemingly secure job may have recurring dreams that reveal a dark underside to their working situation. Or one in a relationship that has grown stale with time may have a startlingly radiant dream of his or her lover that reminds the dreamer why he or she chose that person to begin with. Conversely, one may dream of a work environment different from their own that has a much more positive feel to it, or of a dream-lover who seems able to provide something sorely missing from one's current relationship. The variations are endless, but the common theme is to shake the dreamer into seeing reality for what it is and, at least occasionally, show how it could be different. Those words, "You do not have to live like this!" can be spoken just as forcefully by the language of dreams.

A convincing argument can be made that the more hardheaded we are, the more direct that still, small voice is likely to be with us. That would explain why it was so direct with me. But whether direct or oblique, subtle or insistent, there is something within us or outside us—depending on your beliefs—that keeps our feckless egos from being completely alone and adrift.

VOCATION

"Who do you report to?" If you've spent time in or around corporations, you have heard or asked that question a thousand times. What we mean, of course, is: Who is your boss? Who signs your performance review? Who has the power to promote you or derail you? With the way business concerns are organized, based as they are on the military model of command and control, it means: Who is above you in the chain of command?

But for many, the years of the foundational shifts will turn those questions on their ear, from the extrinsic to the intrinsic. The questions will become more like: Who am I really at my core? How can I find at least some expression of that in my work? What do I really want to be known and remembered for? Do I have what people refer to as a "calling"—and how in the world would I hear it even if I did?

Psychiatrist Roger Gould, writing in the wake of his own second foundational shift, synopsizes the situation very well:

When we are young men, we work primarily out of necessity, to get bigger, and to be part of something that is in itself meaningful. After working for twenty years, we can't work for those reasons predominantly and still stay mentally alive. We must do work that confirms our talents and expresses a psychodynamic theme close to the core of us. Time is too valuable to be spent at a distance from our authentic selves, though we still can't ignore necessity, we're still tempted by rank, and we can temporarily be swept along by a fast-growing organization ... Achieving the right balance may happen slowly, over a period of years, and we may take many missteps before we hit upon the best transformation for us.

It is during such periods that the "still, small voice" can become particularly and insistently focused on our working lives, but if we can hear and heed that call, the voice of vocation can become a most powerful accelerant for a life lived to the full.

The notion of vocation (from the Latin *vocare*, "to call") is really rather subversive to our culture's notions of career development. From high school guidance counselors to career consultants to the batteries of aptitude indicators and skills tests, we tend to take a thoroughly rational approach to what we are "best suited" to do with our lives. There is nothing inherently wrong with any of those things, mind you, but they work best when they are merely helpmates to claiming our strengths, uncovering our weaknesses, and opening our minds to previously undiscovered possibilities.

Vocation is not a rational process. While we may rationally chose a job or even a career, vocation is something that irrationally chooses *us*. And while giving rationality its proper place, to hear that voice of vocation requires us to learn to listen with our non-rational faculties to what a deeper wisdom within us may be trying to say. Attending to our dreams; paying attention to our hunches and gut feelings; sleuthing the patterns of our lives to date; recognizing what manner of things enthuse us and fire our creativity as well as those that suck us dry all are ways of listening to that voice.

We do not find our vocation by listening to the voices that tell us what we "should" or "ought" to do, as well-meaning as such advice may be. We do not find it by adherence to some extrinsic moral or ethical code, no matter how righteous that code might be, else we may find ourselves "faking it" in a way that seems outwardly appealing but is inwardly grinding. And as unseemly as it may be to say this during a time of national recession, we do not find it out of economic necessity or because we invested in training for some specialized path or because we have student loans to repay. That is why the voice of vocation is potentially so subversive. Obedience to a higher—or deeper—calling may not satisfy cultural norms, or the expectations of many around you, or even your own expectations from just a few years earlier.

But in a chapter that has been devoted to things that can either stall us or propel us in our growth, the realization of one's vocation is by far the strongest of propellants. It is difficult to convey what that force can be like unless you have experienced it for yourself. But think, if you will, about those people around you, or about whom you have read who seem to have found it for their own lives.

What you will see is, first, a *passion* for what they do, a palpable energy that seems to flow from some inner source and enlivens all they do. They have a sense of *purpose* that seems to override the peaks and valleys of daily existence. You may often hear them say things like, "I cannot *not* do this. It's like I would shrivel up and die if I didn't. It's that compelling." Yes, it is often true that they appear to be *consumed* by what they do and must take special care of their physical and psychological selves. But as a lifelong teacher now in her late sixties recently said to me, "I have no clue how one is effective in what one does without letting it consume him." And finally, there is a peculiar *optimism* about such folk. It is as if the vagaries of life, its struggles and inevitable setbacks, are now just seen as part of a process that brought them to where they are, and they fully expect that process—complete with struggles and setbacks and joys and grace—to continue.

As that lifelong teacher will attest, it is not always necessary to change careers or even jobs in order to find your vocation. A great many of my business clients have navigated a major foundational shift in their lives and emerged with a greater sense of vitality and purpose for the work they were already doing and the companies for which they were doing it. Inner growth does not always require visible outer change.

Nor does the call of vocation require that you have a traditional job at all. I think of my own mother, who up until the time of her final illness had a consuming passion for her home, family, community, and burgeoning circle of friends. Her energy would sometimes overwhelm those around her (including me), but there is no doubting that her optimism, passion, and creativity touched the lives of many people and left an indelible mark upon them.

In Graham Greene's novel *A Burnt-Out Case*, the chief protagonist, an architect, is reflecting upon the failings of his life and career: "If we really believe in something we have no choice, have we, but to go further. Otherwise life slowly whittles the belief away. My architecture stood still. One can't be a half-believer or a half-architect." People don't begin their life's journey hoping to be a half-assed architect (or lawyer or teacher or mother). But without a sense of vocation, life can whittle us down to a fraction of what we'd hoped for and aspired to. To find your passion in what you do—whatever it is you do—or to have the courage to search until you find it, is the greatest gift you can ever give yourself or those whose lives you touch. From Robert Kegan:

> Passion is its own purpose. Passion can be a bit disdainful of reasonableness and productivity. And passion is among the most sacred and fragile gifts the gods bestow on us. It is fragile before our devastating embarrassment and impatience. And it is sacred because it promises the possibility of new life.

Safe Home

The ancient human question "Who am I?" leads inevitably to the equally important question, "Whose am I?"—Douglas V. Steere

The decisive question for man is: Is he related to something infinite or not? That is the telling question of his life.—Carl Jung

IT TOOK SOME YEARS navigating life's waters, but Tim Geckle has found a personally satisfying answer to the questions asked in the quotes above.

In many ways, Tim's career path was a mirror image of my own. Educated in the Catholic schools of the DC suburbs and armed with a master's in religious education, he seemed set for a career as a teacher. But the reality did not match the "dream" for Tim, and he soon found himself in the midst of his first foundational shift. Part of the resolution of that transition sent him in a direction and toward a career he would never have previously imagined—at age twenty-eight he was on his way to San Francisco to pursue a law degree.

When I met Tim, almost twenty years had passed since that fateful decision. He had become general counsel and a member of the executive committee of one of the largest home builders in the United States. "I love my job," Tim said in our first session, "in spite of the responsibility and the unrelenting pressure to keep proving my value to the company." But I would soon learn that his career journey had not been without its perils and sandbars. He felt compelled to leave the first law firm for which he worked, whose "inhuman and dehumanizing environment" seemed to grind away daily at values he held dear. And even now, having achieved the position to which he had always aspired, Tim would confess to a hidden lack of self-confidence, a tentativeness that seemed to flow out of a realization that his business persona was not always aligned with his private self.

As long as that split existed, Tim could never be as effective outwardly or as comfortable inwardly as he wished and intended to be. For Tim, as long as the answer to the question, "Who am I?" came from the opinions of company superiors or the traditional markers of corporate success, his self-esteem would always remain tentative and his personal power limited.

I last saw Tim in his spacious office in the San Fernando Valley, and much had indeed changed in the ten years I had known him. "Maybe you call it maturity, this business of growing into myself. But the key for me was in being able to reach back and reclaim the qualities I've always known I had and the faith that I was created and put here for a reason. Success—at least the way most people define it—is not the ultimate need I have. I know that I'm a good person of honesty and integrity who cares about others and loves people who care the same way I do. I want to help people and raise good children. I want to continue my search for a greater spiritual life and a deeper relationship with God, and I have absolute faith that if I do those things then I will be successful because that *is* success. I don't have to be shy or tentative or posturing or put you down so that I can somehow feel superior. I have a completely different yardstick for my self-image now."

And for what it's worth, that approach to life has paid huge dividends at work. While his title has not changed, a case can be made that Tim is the number two man in the company, a powerful and able confidant of the CEO.

The story doesn't end there. Tim would say it was just another beginning. For the past several years, Tim has been taking the necessary steps and coursework for ordination as a priest. His intention is to test the waters of full-time ministry once he leaves corporate America for good. While I have personally always believed (as my book *The Congruent Life* argues) that such a calling could be answered while still deeply ensconced in the business world, Tim is satisfied that this may be the next logical step in his life and career—and his own personal answer to the question "To whom to you report?"

THE "BIDDINGS OF HEAVEN"

There are not a lot of "Tims" out there. I'm not one either. But what we do know about the foundational shifts is that the resolution of each shift can have profound implications for our spirituality. That is by no means a recent or a cultural phenomenon. Many centuries ago, Confucius wrote about the same developmental dynamic in fifth-century BCE China: "At thirty, I had planted my feet firm upon the ground. At forty, I no longer suffered from perplexities. At fifty, I knew what were the biddings of heaven. At sixty, I heard them with a docile ear."

The truth is, the experiences of any age or stage of life can prepare us for a deepening of our spiritual selves. But it is in the wrestling and resolution of life's foundational shifts that the ground for spiritual development becomes most fertile. We suffer, and in suffering we often find the source of deeper strength. We recognize the limitations—yea, even the smallness—of our own egos and begin to look for greater meaning outside of their narrow constraints. We discover our dependence upon and connectedness to others and begin to live out that realization with a new selflessness. We discover—or rediscover—who we truly are at our core and determine to live out of that central place with the help of spiritual disciplines that have outlived time.

For some, an awakened spirituality may mean a return to one's traditional religious roots; others may find this new hunger met best by something completely new. For me, I always figured I would grow best in the soil in which I was originally planted. And so, while appreciating the living reality of which all the world's great religions speak, I found myself nourished by my Christian faith, particularly during the tumult of my midlife foundational shift. I just came to see the old stories and symbols of Christianity with new eyes. My childhood faith, like Tim's, came alive again for me in a radically different way.

As Jung was wont to point out, the renewal of our spiritual natures is not just a "nice" outcome of the developmental process, it can be your saving grace. In one of Jung's most oft-quoted passages, he makes the point starkly:

Among all my patients in the second half of life—that is to say, over thirty-five—there has not been one whose problem in the last resort was not that of finding a religious outlook on life. It is safe to say that every one of them fell ill because he had lost what the living religions of every age have given to their followers, and none of them has been really healed who did not regain his religious outlook.

To Jung, that "religious outlook" did not require allegiance to a particular creed or membership in a church. "It is much more a question," he wrote, "of his quite irrational need for what we call a spiritual life, and this he cannot obtain from universities, libraries, or even from churches. He cannot accept what these have to offer because it touches only his head but does not stir his heart."

Stirring, and shaking, are what the foundational shifts of life do best.

What "Transformation" Really Is

"All our words from loose using have lost their edge," complained that great master of words Ernest Hemingway. Or, as I argued in *The Congruent Life*, a word that has become so popularized as to mean too many things to too many people ends up meaning nothing at all. Such is the fate of the word "transformation." A high-sounding and vaulted noun to be sure—but what does it really mean in the context of human growth and maturation?

Throughout the pages of this book we have talked time and again about the choices, challenges, and conflicts that come as we move from one stage of life to another. In the most critical phases of such transitions, we even use words such as "torn" or "split apart" to describe how we feel. What we are saying, in essence, is that we feel conflicted by two alternatives that cannot simultaneously be pursued—we must choose one. We are saying we feel sundered between two realities that cannot coexist indefinitely. One must win out.

Since the ancients, mankind has understood this to be the way the human mind works. We are hopelessly dualistic creatures, and to a certain extent that is how it *must* be for us to make sense of our world. We only understand "hot" because there is something called "cold."

Light is only understood as light because we experience darkness. Love is to be treasured because its opposites are fear and hatred.

But could it be that in the most important moments of our lives, willing an answer from among two irreconcilable opposites is not what is required? Instead of *re*solving a split through our own grit and determination, is it possible to *dis*solve the split? Is it possible that between that rock and that hard place there exists a third, unthought-of alternative, which must be lived into rather than logically computed?

Yes. And that is what personal transformation really is. Jung offered this psychological explanation for what happens in the transformation process:

> In the psychology of the individual there is always, at such moments, an agonizing situation of conflict from which there seems to be no way out—at least for the conscious mind ... But out of this collision of opposites the unconscious psyche always creates a third thing of an irrational nature, which the conscious mind neither expects nor understands. It presents itself in a form that is neither a straight "yes" nor a straight "no" and is consequently rejected by both. For the conscious mind knows nothing beyond the opposites and, as a result, has no knowledge of the thing that unites them. Since, however, the solution of the conflict through the union of opposites is of vital importance, and is moreover the very thing that the conscious mind is longing for, some inkling of the creative act, and of the significance of it, nevertheless gets through.

But Jung also offered a religious explanation: "If all goes well, the solution, seemingly of its own accord, appears out of nature. Then and then only is it convincing. It is felt as 'grace.'" And Grace is precisely how my clients—and I—would describe it.

In the first rumblings of a foundational shift, our choices seem both stark and confusing. Do I keep the security of this stultifying job or do I try for a breakout into something new? Do I try to salvage this marriage, or do I pursue the new relationship I've found? Yes, conscious choices have to be made, and they are often wrenching. But almost everyone I know who has navigated a major life shift has reported experiencing a process by which they lived into a solution that actually changed the original questions. And for those with a spiritual orientation, they confess in unison a belief that God was directly involved in that process. In fact, the experience of "grace" in that form, at such a critical time in their lives, brought many of them intimately closer to their religious and spiritual roots.

Jung used the term "transcendent function" to refer to that process outside our conscious understanding whereby a conflict of opposites engenders new and unforeseen growth. No matter what obstacle life places in our path, provided only it be a difficult one, it creates the setting in which true transformation becomes possible. But because transcendence "cannot be contrived by reason, it can only be created through living," it takes time. Fortunately, the foundational shifts pay little attention to our notions of efficiency, and transformation has as much time as it needs.

This process, as it unfolds over time, is captured nicely by Raymond Studzinski, whose book *Spiritual Direction and Midlife Development* is an essential tool for anyone seeking to understand the religious implications of the transcendent function.

> Transformational knowing begins in an experience of conflict when previous ways of knowing begin to break down. It is a phenomenon similar to that which confronts a person who is trying to solve a puzzle. When attempts at solving the puzzle based on one's usual interpretive schemes fail, the *second* step finds people scanning the field of possibilities for a new perspective while they continue to be challenged by the conflict. This scanning, which relies heavily on the imagination, is both a conscious and unconscious process. *Thirdly*, an intuition or insight which gives a clue to the resolution of the conflict appears on the boundary between the unconscious and the conscious as a result of the constructive act of the imagination. It is by this central act that the elements of the ruptured situation are *transformed*, and a new perception, perspective, or world view is bestowed on the knower. With the appearance of the insight, the knower experiences a surge of energy—energy which was formerly absorbed within the conflict. Release from the conflict in this *fourth* step gives rise to self-transcendence. The new insight makes possible *finally* a reinterpretation of the problem

situation. A new vision is applied to the former conflict and to a corresponding world view.

The "surge of energy" that comes with this process is invaluable. It is as if the obstacle created by the conflict has dammed up all of life's energies, which continue to mound up and pool on the near side of the dam. Life feels stuck and stagnant, yet one can still feel the roiling tension of waters looking for a place to burst forth. When that finally happens—when the resolution finally comes—it feel less like a bursting of the dam than that the water has found a way around it; a new gradient down which to rush and tumble, creating a whole new stream bed as it goes. These are some of the most exciting and creative times of our lives—and one of God's greatest gifts.

INDIVIDUATION—A ROSE BY ANY OTHER NAME

Jung coined a word for this transformational process that has passed into common parlance—"individuation." It means becoming an individual, undivided, embracing our incomparable uniqueness and our innermost realities. We "individuate" to the extent that we become our true selves.

But it is not an insular process. Indeed, we are surprised to find that our conscious egos, which serve us so faithfully in the main, are not at the center of this process at all and affect it only to the extent that they provide cooperation or create obstacles.

Jung was a scientist, and though prone to lengthy forays into the worlds of philosophy and religion, he tried to use objective language to describe his observations. One such word, critical to understanding Jung's psychology, is the "self." Jung observed that while we all like to think that our well-constructed ego is the master and center of our personal universe, life will time and again teach us it isn't so. There is a vast sea of unconscious material within us, whose surface we may occasionally sail but whose depths are completely unknown. There are those distasteful parts of ourselves (our "shadow") that have been consigned to the dungeon under lock and key but will occasionally break loose in the form of anger, lust, or other unseemly behavior. There are our contrasexual tendencies we have sloughed off to the other gender but which return in the anima dreams of a man or the animus dreams of a woman. (For a discussion of the shadow, anima, and animus, see the preceding chapter.)

But the aspect of our psyche most difficult to define is the *self*. In one sense it is a circle whose circumference encompasses everything else—and certainly our egos. In another way, it can be seen as a unifying center, an organizing principle that seems to have goals and purposes of its own. As Jung admits, "Intellectually the self is no more than a psychological concept, a construct that serves to express an unknowable essence which we cannot grasp as such, since by definition it transcends our powers of comprehension."

But then Jung goes on to say what those with a religious orientation would have guessed: "It might equally well be called the 'God within us.' The beginnings of our whole psychic life seem to be inextricably rooted in this point, and all our highest and ultimate purposes seem to be striving toward it. This paradox is unavoidable, as always, when we try to define something that lies beyond the bourn of our understanding."

This is among the most controversial aspects of Jung's psychology, but it might just as well evoke a "duh!" from believers of the world's great religions. That paradoxical center and circumference of the human psyche, that reality we cannot fully describe but to which we seem innately to strive, the "still, small voice" within is nothing less than the immanent nature of God.

This is why I argued in *The Congruent Life* that the process of individuation and spiritual growth were, at bottom, the same thing. Gradually over the course of our lifetime—but with opportunity for acceleration during the foundational shifts—the conscious ego is confronted with its limitations and begins to sense the reality that lies beyond its bounds. Jung believed that the goal of individuation, and thus our greatest hope for achieving personal authenticity, was in building up the connection between the temporal ego and the larger reality of the self. The whole of depth psychology can be understood as the process of intentionally creating and strengthening this alignment. It is also, many would assert, the psychological version of Paul's famous declaration, "It is no longer I who live, but Christ who lives within me" (Galatians 2:20).

But if this were as easy as it sounds on the surface, someone would have figured a way to bottle and sell it by now. It is not easy, for the principal reason that the ego can have an extraordinarily difficult time giving in to the notion that it is not the center of its own universe. Having been carefully constructed, pruned, and preened over the course of life's early decades, the ego is now being asked to surrender—or at least share—its primacy. Jung described it this way: "Although it is able to preserve its structure, the ego is ousted from its central and dominating position and thus finds itself in the role of a passive observer who lacks the power to assert his will ... In this way the will, as disposable energy, gradually subordinates itself to the stronger factor, namely to the new totality-figure I call the *self*."

Life's external circumstances may be "hard." But they are mere annoyances compared to the inner path and perils of individuation. Some are overwhelmed and retreat to the comfort of the known. At least as often, the ego will sense the emergence of the greater reality within and try to claim it as its own—a very dangerous condition called inflation. In this way the ego can retain the illusion of mastery by seeing the wisdom and transformative power of the self as something the ego possesses, but has only recently discovered. You may see such inflated egos on the front page of the morning paper; but you don't have to look any further to find them than to the merely insufferable bores you encounter day to day. Jesus said, "Many are called, but few are chosen" (Matthew 22:14). I always wondered if that was because few really *wanted* to be chosen.

But this much is certain: for those who actively pursue the path of individuation, there is a broadening of the personality, an enrichment and depth that comes from reclaiming the gold from what was lost or banished during the decades of ego building. We open ourselves up to the inner forces that can bring about true "transformation"—the new ways of thinking and being that can rise from our seemingly hopeless dilemmas. As we chip through the brittle crusts of our egos, we often discover whole new worlds—or single solitary souls—in need of what we uniquely have to give. And for those with a strong spiritual orientation, it is a way of coming to God from the inside out, without in any way diminishing the value of group worship, sacrament and scripture in the care of the soul.

True Contentment

"I just want to be happy." How many times have you heard that wishful plea from someone you know, or even uttered it yourself? What we mean by that, of course, is that our current situation is quite *un*happy, and we yearn for a time in the future when that will change.

But is that the state to which we really aspire? The primary definition of happy in Webster's Collegiate Dictionary is "favored by luck or fortune," yet the world is full of people "favored" with good looks, status, and money who seem distinctly unhappy. On the other hand, we've all seen those whose external circumstances were so limited and limiting that it would crush our spirits if we were in their place, yet they still exhibit a kind of "joy" and "gladness" (Webster's two other synonyms for "happy").

Perhaps what we seek instead is *contentment.* To be contented is to be satisfied with oneself and one's circumstances, whatever they may be. It means that one's possessions are enough, one's status sufficient, one's life satisfactory. Coming from the Latin word *continere,* meaning "to hold in or contain," contentment says that we hold within the bounds of our life all that is needful. Yes, we will have our worries and anxieties like everyone else, but we contain the essential. As opposed to the transitory nature of happiness and its reliance upon good fortune, contentment is like a song we can call to memory at any moment or a ring that never leaves our finger. Contentment is about what *is,* while happiness is all too often about what we want life to be "just as soon as" we can get out of school, or exit this job, or get married, or finalize the divorce, or snag that winning lottery ticket.

So from whence, pray tell, comes contentment? The exigencies of our individual makeup do have to be given their due here. Some of us are just more optimistic and resilient by nature than others. Moreover, we can have psychological spots on our souls which can make contentment more elusive, as for the narcissistic, the avaricious, and those with pathologically deep-seated insecurities.

But for most of us, much will depend on how ably and courageously we have traversed life's foundational shifts. To use the shorthand we have employed before for these complex life events, how well have we wrested our own life and values from the collective systems that surrounded us? How well did we examine and redefine our lives and careers in midlife? How carefully did we unpack and repack our bags for the journey of life's third shift?

What we know is that for every stage of life mangled or mismanaged, the next will be more challenging. For every transition brushed past or glossed over, there will be hell to pay in the next. And for every time you become frozen in place, taking shelter in the status quo out of fear of the unknown, life will continue to pelt you with the same unresolved issues until you either move forward or—far worse—are left to your own self-chosen fate.

For those of you who have encountered and faced a foundational shift, you know that the way is anything but smooth and the work anything but easy. Reading the stories of the people in this book will tell you that much. And having lived those stories along with those people, I can tell you with certainty that there were times of doubt and reversals and just plain nuttiness. But while very few of these folks were artists in the traditional sense, each was drawing upon his or her own unique canvas and trying to create a work of art that might be called *A Life Well Lived*. As Jung once said, "the art of life is the most distinguished and rarest of all the arts. Who ever succeeded in draining the whole cup with grace?"

But in decades now of watching those artworks unfold (and looking at my own canvas, filled as it is with erasures and "do-overs"), it is clear there are several aspects to this state of mind we call contentment. Let's call them the Blessings of Maturity. They are the manifestations of contentment which come to us when we live into, and through, those times in life when the very ground beneath us shakes.

Selfhood. People who have been through the wars of growth and self-discovery know their own terrain pretty well. They have uncovered their gifts and special skills, just as they have shined the light of awareness on their soft spots and foibles. They have faced adversity and know how they tend to react to it. They know what works for them and what doesn't. All of this can lead to a realistic sense of self-worth that depends less on the measurements and agendas of others and more upon their own realization of what they do and do not do well. They can stand alone and they can stand in peace with others. They know where the sandbars in the river are, and now, at long last, they have both the will and the knowledge to avoid them. They may no longer dream the fanciful dreams of youth but have the energy and enthusiasm to pursue the mature versions of those dreams—and altogether new ones—into a future that promises to be enlivening and exciting. Chronic self-doubt has given way to self-reflection, while bravado has given up its place to a quiet self-confidence.

None of this would have been possible if they had not been required, of necessity, to plumb their own depths, to root out their unproductive patterns, and to piece together effective ones. They encountered boulders in the path, and like some insidious vine, grew around them. If we stick with own "first principles" and do not learn the art of adaptation, we might still think of ourselves as unalterably and inflexibly "right," while the rest of the world might rightly see us as rigid and small.

It is not pride so much as it is acceptance of the person we essentially are and how we became that way. Perhaps it is the kind of contentment of which W. B. Yeats caught a short glimpse (see his poem, which begins our chapter on the third shift) when he said, "It seemed so great, my happiness / that I was blessed—and could bless."

Community. In the introduction we described a kind of choreography of life. We waltz, with at least some degree of predictability, between periods of stability and transition, between times of secure embeddedness in a group and times when only a more individual, solitary way will do. One who has worked through a foundational shift in life will recognize this pattern immediately.

But that pattern is not just a reality of the human maturation process. One cannot read Joseph Campbell's classic *The Hero with a Thousand Faces* without realizing that the same theme is fundamental to any heroic myth, tale, or story. From Moses to George Washington to Dorothy in *The Wizard of Oz*, the hero must foray far from the comfortable protection of the group, there to encounter perils and experiences that initiate a new way of thinking and being. But the story is never over until the hero returns to the community, where he or she bestows the gifts that were won in solitude. Put in psychological language, "The individual can individuate only alone; that the fruits of one's creativity can be bestowed on the collective, but only after they have been won in solitary effort."

We tend to think of contentment as something nicely nestled down deep inside those who possess it—something like their own private treasure. But both history and the experience of others tells me that is not so. In our three rather random examples, Moses emerges from his initiation in Sinai a completely different person from the impetuous young man who had killed an Egyptian guard, and he is held in esteem by three of the world's greatest religions. Washington's early life held no clue of the statesman he would become, but seven years of war and the struggles of a young republic forged perhaps America's greatest leader. Even Dorothy shared a new appreciation of love and home with those around her upon her return.

In ways that were different but just as important for their communities, you can see how the "heroes" whose stories fill the pages of this book survived major transitions in their lives and careers, only to take back into their families, workplaces, and communities the fruits of what they had learned. As Jung put it, "Individuation does not shut one out from the world but gathers the world to oneself."

Forgiveness. One of the most freeing things a human being can do is to forgive himself. That doesn't mean making excuses or finding ways to blame others—or upbringing, or circumstance—for our misdeeds. It means to own the totality of who we are and have discovered ourselves to be through ruthless self-examination, without having those revelations cripple our future. "You need to claim the events in your life to make yourself yours," wrote Florida Scott Maxwell. "When you truly possess all you have been and done, which may take some time, you are fierce with reality."

I like that phrase "fierce with reality" because self-forgiveness is not about being soft on yourself or taking an easy way out. It is, as T. S. Eliot put it poetically, "the shame / Of motives late revealed, and the awareness / Of things ill done and done to others' harm / Which once you took for exercise of virtue." It is staring reality straight in the face and yet refusing to let the past shackle the future.

In contentment, the war is over. There have been defeats; there have been victories. There have been shameful times and shining moments. Much has been lost but much more has been won. The treaty has been signed and the troops have stood down. That which is done is done. But the one spoil of war irrevocably possessed is your own self-chosen future, enriched by what the past has taught.

"Harrowing," a poem by Parker Palmer, expresses the thought most eloquently:

The plow has savaged this sweet field
Misshapen clods of earth kicked up
Rocks and twisted roots exposed to view
Last year's growth demolished by the blade.
I have plowed my life this way
Turned over a whole history
Looking for the roots of what went wrong
Until my face is ravaged, furrowed, scarred.

Enough. The job is done.
Whatever's been uprooted, let it be
Seedbed for the growing that's to come.
I plowed to unearth last year's reasons—

The farmer plows to plant a greening season.

Stability. From the point of view of external occurrences, life's second half doesn't seem to offer much in the way of stability. Ailments and "procedures" begin to mount. When job losses occur they can be more devastating. People often have to learn to live with less. Long-term marriages can sunder. We lose loved ones to death or suffer the ingratitude of the living.

But in weathering life's transitions, something like a central core builds up in us. It consists of the strengths that have been forged, the uniqueness and gifts claimed, and the countless little ways in which we have grown into a more authentic version of ourselves. And that central core is now capable of weathering a great many of life's vicissitudes. One of the blessings of maturity is that no loss can completely defeat us, no circumstance can completely dislodge us, and no illness can completely separate us from that essential core. We have learned through challenges and reversals that we have, somewhere within us, the strength to withstand them. They can chip away at us, but they can never render our lives hopeless or meaningless. Some sort of rock has been formed, and mere misfortune is no match for it.

Perhaps the best way to understand that central core is to look around at the people who don't have it—and there are far too many of them out there. Of them, Roger Gould offers this depressing assessment: "they cling to the childhood consciousness view that power and status are an index of human worth. As reversals occur to such people with increasing frequency as they age, they perceive themselves as losing the battle of life. They begin to attack life itself as meaningless as they slide downhill. Their envies and jealousies become larger, like warts on the nose, as their humanity shrinks."

I always like to think there is hope for such people; but the truth is that if they have not found their inner core through the hard work of navigating life's foundational shifts, their latter years are a difficult place to start.

Faith. As you know from these pages, I deeply believe that human growth and development can lead directly to a greater spirituality and to an opportunity for a more personal relationship with God. But neither belief in a supreme being—much less in a particular creed or religion—is necessary for the kind of faith I speak of here. If you navigate life's foundational shifts "well enough" and for long enough, a kind of faith in the process itself emerges.

Try this. Think about the times when you were dead set on a particular path and were applying all your cunning and willpower in order to achieve it, but you "failed." The job or the relationship or the venture just didn't pan out. Of course, you were devastated at the time. But in time, how often did you realize that it was really the wrong path for you? Or, perhaps, did something else take its place in your life that turned out to be richer and fuller than that at which you "failed"? Or think about a time when you were struggling to find your way, only to have the "right" person or book or teacher or experience open a door for you that you didn't even know existed. Perhaps you have been on the horns of a dilemma, feeling split in half by two seemingly irreconcilable choices, only to experience the kind of "transformation" we spoke of earlier in this chapter.

"Now faith is the substance of things hoped for, the evidence of things not seen," says the writer of the Epistle to the Hebrews. (Hebrews 11:1, KJV). We don't have to know *why* it happens; life simply teaches us that it *does*. We may describe the patterns and apparent purposefulness of life in words that include God, or we may choose not to, but its cohesiveness remains. It is one of the greatest gifts of maturity to be relieved of the notion that everything depends on us and the power of our will.

Contentment consists, at least in part, in the experiential knowledge that having faith enough to let go of our willfulness is at least as much of a virtue as dogged determination. In the economy of life's changes, it is probably the more valuable currency.

Integrity. To groundbreaking psychologist Erik Erikson, only those who traversed life's cycles could enjoy its crowning achievement, which he called "integrity." As Erikson uses the word, integrity has nothing to do with adherence to a particular moral code or the esteem in which one is held by others. Lacking a succinct definition, he points instead to the attributes of one who possesses integrity:

> It is the acceptance of one's own and only life cycle and of the people who have become significant to it as something that had to be and that, by necessity, permitted of no substitutions. It thus means a new different love of one's parents, free of the wish that they should have been different, and the acceptance of the fact that one's life is one's own responsibility. It is a sense of comradeship with men and women of distant times and of different pursuits, who have created orders and objects and sayings conveying human dignity and love. Although aware of the relativity of all the various life styles which have given meaning to human striving, the possessor of integrity is ready to defend the dignity of his own life style against all physical and economic threats.

Contentment means not only the ability to forgive oneself, but it means the ability—indeed the necessity—of forgiving others. It is instructive that the word "integrity" derives from the same Latin root as our word "entire," meaning "whole" and "having no element or part left out." To possess integrity in the Eriksonian sense is to leave nothing out, whether it is one's own foibles, the wounds we suffered at the hands of others, or the shortcomings of our parents. We accept the sum total of our life's experience not just because it *is* but because it *had to be*. To wish it were otherwise would be to enviously wish we had someone else's life, when the one life we have to live—and have the responsibility to live well against all threats—is our own.

While inexact in his definition of integrity, Erikson was clear about how he thought its opposite would appear. When the "one and only life cycle" was not accepted and traversed, Erikson saw the clinical result as despair and disgust. "Despair expresses the feeling that the time is short, too short for the attempt to start another life and try out alternative roads to integrity. Such a despair is often hidden behind a show of disgust, a misanthropy, or a chronic contemptuous displeasure with particular institutions and particular people—a disgust and a displeasure which … only signify the individual's contempt of himself."

The choice of integrity over despair was, for Erikson, the ultimate fruit of the life-cycle process and the gift of a life well lived.

Home. In one sense of the word, my home no longer exists. The house in which I was raised is under a four-lane highway. The school that held such memories for me is itself only a memory, long ago razed to make way for a new one. The pretty white-frame church where my parents were married and I worshiped is now nothing but a parking lot for the much larger (and substantially uglier) brick edifice next door. Such is the result of unrestrained development and the passage of half a century!

But while it is helpful to have touchstones of our youth to remind us of home, it is not altogether necessary—a good thing since the average American family moves at least once every five years.

When you allow yourselves to think deeply and quietly about it, what does home really mean to you? What does it take to make you feel "at home"? Who is there? What are the attributes of the people you would *like* to be there? What are your surroundings like and why did you (would you) pick them? Do they have a particularly comforting or comfortable quality about them, and why? What are the activities you most enjoy there, and in what ways do they nourish you? Is there a particular geography or landscape to the setting and why did you (or would you) choose it? What makes you feel safe?

Most people can fashion answers to those questions. But the more of life's cycles we have traversed, the more important those answers become. At the onset of our maturity, no matter who we are or where we've been, the desire to feel "at home" becomes compelling. Like

Odysseus, we may have metaphorically spent decades at war and at sea. We yearn for the streets of our native Ithaca, the touch of the faithful Penelope, and the companionship of the son we never really knew, now grown to manhood. The memories of Trojan horses and terrifying shipwrecks will forever be part of who we are and have become, but we would rather tell our grandchildren stories about them than relive them.

Here's the catch: if you haven't carefully examined the values and expectations that you imported from your youth—an important task of life's first foundational shift—you will find it difficult to discern what you need to make your home uniquely and satisfyingly yours. You may be one of those people who yearns for nothing more than to move back into your parents' house once they are gone, sleep in your childhood bed, and reminisce. Without the redefinition and redirection that comes from midlife, you may have a nagging feeling that your home, as comfortable or stylish as it may be, doesn't quite fit you. Your house, like your life, belongs in some ways to someone else. And, of course, only those who have faced the task of "leaving in and leaving out," required by the third foundational shift, can commit to the places, pursuits, and even people who will be part of their mature years.

In one sense it is really rather simple. In order to be contented you must know what contents you. In order to know what truly contents you, you must have gone through the purging, winnowing, and reclamation projects that are the foundational shifts of life.

In the United States, people rank happiness as their most important goal. Ironically, however, recent studies have shown that the more value people place on happiness, the more unhappy and depressed they tend to become. Perhaps the old saying is true: seek happiness, and you will never find happiness; seek contentment and you may well find yourself contented—with happiness thrown in to boot.

Your Next Chapter

Go confidently in the direction of your dreams. Live the life you have imagined.—Henry David Thoreau

IN ONE OF THE well-worn stories of the Judeo-Christian Bible, a group of "wise men" (the Magi) set out from their kingdoms in the east on a great adventure. Following a mysterious and beautiful star, they traveled a great distance to bestow earthly gifts upon one they thought to be a new and different kind of king. The story can be told to you by almost any child in any Christian Sunday school class anywhere.

But this was only the first half of their journey. Do you recall what happened in the second half? King Herod had set a trap. The Magi were to return to Herod and let him know of the child's location so that he too could "worship" him. In the cryptic confines of Matthew 2:12, we learn that the Wise Men were warned in a dream not to fall for the plot but to "go home by another way."

Without the warning, or the heeding of the warning, or if the Wise Men had been a bit less wise, we can fairly speculate what would have happened. As foreign dignitaries, the Magi would have been welcomed into Herod's palace, feted, and entreated to stay. There would have been feasts and toasts, honors bestowed, and gifts exchanged.

But sooner or later some nasty rumor would have started. Perhaps the Magi were not being sufficiently forthcoming with all they knew about this young king. Indeed they must be spies from the empires lying to the east. They would have been prevented from leaving while the interrogations continued, eventually imprisoned, and likely killed. No "safe home" at the hands of King Herod.

There is a lesson here for us. The first half of our journey can indeed be a great adventure, full of wonders and discoveries. We follow the star—whatever that is for us—sometimes so far that home for us is a distant memory. This is as it should be.

But if we assume that the track of the second half is the same as the first, we are subject to fatal error. If we do not heed the warnings of our most insistent inner voices that are telling us to go home by another way, we may find ourselves stuck in Herod's palace. Oh, it may seem at first a wonderful place to be, what with all the trappings of wealth and possessions of power and the temporary sense of security. But its price is a gilded imprisonment, a stagnation of life, and eventually life's end.

It is a lot easier to grow older than it is to grow wiser, isn't it? In the pages of this book, we have followed the stories of men and women who have encountered one of life's three crucial transitions. Some floundered or failed. Many spent lonely, learning time in the desert before emerging to a richer and more authentic life. Others seem to have more easily drained the whole cup with grace.

But one cannot help but notice the presence (or absence) of three important factors that account for their varying degrees of success.

The first is *insight*—a growing knowledge of themselves, their hidden motivations, and the forces that were at work within them. That insight could have been hard won through trial and error. It could have come from the accumulated wisdom of parents, counselors, and friends. Who knows? Maybe it came from a book such as this one. But that insight gave them a grounded sense of where they were in life's journey and what would be required to move forward.

The second is *patience*. There are no "Road to Damascus" experiences for most of us, and illumination does not come in a blinding flash of light. Personal growth is painfully slow. Indeed, we had best get used to the fact that it will last an entire lifetime. Patience, here, is like the farmer who plants the furrowed fields in springtime. We must wait upon life's timing for life's bounty, even as we know that it will take our own hard work and sweat to bring the crop to harvest.

Finally, it takes *courage*. There are always powerful forces arrayed against change. There is the forward inertia that, as with Taylor Gattis, keeps us rocketing in the same direction, or the torpid inertia of a Sarah Beeson that keeps us mired in the same place. And there are the Voices—you "can't", you "ought not", it's "not realistic"—that come both from within us and from those around us. As we observed at the beginning of this book, it is a difficult thing for a bird to be hatched from its shell—even more difficult for it to learn to fly. But the alternative is not that attractive. Courage, it seems, is not the absence of fear or reserve, it is the knowledge that there is something far more important than your fear and reserve.

Insight, patience, and courage are words that easily come to mind when I think about Claudia. I first met this energetic fifty-year-old when she was a program participant at Greensboro's Center for Creative Leadership. She flounced into my office for our one-hour feedback session and announced that she wanted to tell me her "life story." I'm sure I looked nervously at my watch before saying, "I'm afraid we only have an hour together today."

"That's fine," she shot back, "this will only take a minute or two. It's the story of my life in five short chapters."

Oh great, I thought as I settled back into my chair. *This session isn't a minute old and my client has already hijacked it!*

But what I heard next would stick with me for a long time to come. Fortunately, as was our practice at CCL, the story was recorded verbatim:

"Chapter 1: I am walking down a road. There is an enormous hole in the road. I fall in the hole. And it's not my fault, you see. The city should have put up some sort of barricade. In any event it takes me a hell of a long time to crawl out.

"Chapter 2: I'm walking down the same road. I forget the hole is there. I fall in again. It's still not my fault because the city still hasn't put up a barricade. It takes me a long time to get out.

"Chapter 3: I am walking down the same road with the same hole. I know the hole is there but I fall in again. It's like I can't help myself.

Okay, so I know it's my fault, and this time I'm able to scramble put pretty quickly.

"Chapter 4: I'm walking down the same road with the same hole in it. Only this time I walk around the hole." [long pause]

"That's great," I said, "but I thought you said there were five chapters."

"There are," she said with a wide grin. "In Chapter 5 I take a completely different road! Who wants to go down one with a big hole in it?"

Thus was born a friendship and correspondence that lasted long after her return to her native Iowa. Claudia had arrived at a place in her life where she could clearly see the holes into which she had habitually fallen. There were serial relationships after a failed marriage, all of which ended in disappointment. And there were serial jobs, all of which started with high expectations but ground down to dead-end despair. Insight often comes painfully.

By her own reckoning, it took Claudia a good six years to understand the first four chapters of her "life story." "There were a lot of dark moments during those years," she recalled, "but I had faith that if I were patient enough, something would break. The alternative, after all, was just falling into the same damned hole."

It took courage for Claudia to enter into a new relationship, and (as I can attest) it takes at least that much courage to start one's own business. But eventually she did both. She now likes to brag that it is only an "eleven-second commute" from the bedroom she shares with her husband, Calvin, to her upstairs office, from whence she oversees a growing regional business.

"I took a completely different road," says Claudia, reflecting back on our first meeting, "and, I mean, I *had to*. No amount of trying to fill those holes in or learning how to avoid them was going to change the fact that it was an old potholed road that was full of old traps. Life had another way in mind for me. I had to find it and follow it."

Insight, patience, and courage had forged a "wise woman" indeed.

Nothing is known of the Wise Men after their safe return to the kingdoms of the east. One can imagine that they brought back with them a cache of stories and experiences infinitely more valuable than the gifts they laid at the feet of Jesus. Perhaps there were other penultimate adventures in store for them. I hope so. But none of that would have been possible if they had not, like Claudia, obeyed the laws of life's "return trip," and gone home by another way.

As should you.

References

Introduction

Eliot, T. S., *Four Quartets* (New York: Harcourt Brace Jovanovich, 1943), 39.

Erikson, Erik H., *Identity and the Life Cycle* (New York: Norton, 1980).

Hollis, James, *The Middle Passage: From Misery to Meaning in Midlife* (Toronto: Inner City Books, 1993), 23.

Jung, C. G., *Alchemical Studies* (Princeton, NJ: Princeton University Press, 1967), 15.

Kaplan, Robert E., *Beyond Ambition: How Driven Managers Can Lead Better and Live Better* (San Francisco: Jossey-Bass, Inc.,1991).

Kegan, Robert, *The Evolving Self: Problem and Process in Human Development* (Cambridge, Mass.: Harvard University Press, 1982).

Levinson, Daniel J., *The Season's of a Man's Life* (New York: Ballantine, 1978).

Stein, Murray, *In Midlife* (Putnam, Conn.: Spring Publications, Inc., 1983).

Thompson, C. Michael, *The Congruent Life: Following the Inward Path to Fulfilling Work and Inspired Leadership* (San Francisco: Jossey-Bass, 2000).

The First Shift: Into Your Own

Eliot, *Four Quartets*, 17.

Erikson, Erik H., *Childhood and Society* (New York: Norton, 1963), 263.

Hollis, *The Middle Passage*, 19–20, 24.

Jung, *The Symbolic Life* (Princeton, NJ: Princeton University Press, 1969), 263.

_____, *The Structure and Dynamics of the Psyche* (Princeton, NJ: Princeton University Press, 1960), 392.

_____, *Memories, Dreams, Reflections* (New York: Vintage Books, 1965), 140.

Kegan, Robert, *In Over Our Heads: The Mental Demands of Modern Life* (Cambridge, MA: Harvard University Press, 1994).

Levinson, *The Seasons of a Man's Life*, 58, 199.

Palmer, Parker J., *Let Your Life Speak: Listening for the Voice of Vocation* (San Francisco: Jossey-Bass, 2000), 2–3.

The Second Shift: Down at the Crossroads

Eliot, *Four Quartets*, 26.

Fitzgerald, Catherine, *Developing Leaders: Research and Applications in Psychological Type and Leadership Development* (Palo Alto, CA: Davies-Black Publishing, 1997), 315.

Handy, Charles, *The Age of Paradox* (Cambridge, MA: Harvard Business School Press, 1994), 50.

Hollis, *The Middle Passage*, 13, 66, 95.

Johnson, Robert A., *Living Your Unlived Life: Coping with Unrealized Dreams and Fulfilling Your Purpose in the Second Half of Life* (New York: Tarcher/Penguin, 2007), 63–4.

Jung, *The Structure and Dynamics of the Psyche*, 395–400.

____, *Two Essays on Analytical Psychology* (Princeton, NJ: Princeton University Press, 1953), 75.

Kegan, *The Evolving Self*, 231.

Leslie, Jean B. and Van Velsor, Ellen, *A Look at Derailment Today: North America and Europe* (Greensboro, NC: Center for Creative Leadership, 1996), 32.

Levinson, *The Seasons of a Man's Life*, 62.

Ortega y Gasset, Jose, *Man and Crisis* (New York: Norton, 1958).

Quinn, Robert E., *Deep Change: Discovering the Leader Within* (San Francisco: Jossey-Bass, 1996), 66.

Sheehy, Gail, *New Passages: Mapping Your Life Across Time* (New York: Ballantine, 1995), 3–5.

The Third Shift: Leaning into Life

ABC News, "Edwards Admits Sexual Affair; Lied as Presidential Candidate," http://abcnews.go.com/Blotter/Story?id=5441195.

Beebe, John, *Integrity in Depth* (College Station, TX: Texas A&M University Press, 1992), 6.

Brehony, Kathleen A., *Awakening at Midlife* (New York: Riverhead Books, 1996), 243.

Freedman, Marc, *Encore: Finding Work that Matters in the Second Half of Life* (Cambridge, MA: Perseus, 2007).

Goethe, Johann Wolfgang von, in Levinson, *The Seasons of a Man's Life*, 247.

Handy, *Waiting for the Mountain to Move: Reflections on Work and Life* (San Francisco: Jossey-Bass, 1999), 99, 133.

_____, *The Age of Paradox*, 50.

Hillman, James, *The Soul's Code: In Search of Character and Calling* (New York: Random House, 1996), 6, 135.

James, William, Letter to his wife Alice Gibbons James, 1878.

Jung, *Memories, Dreams, Reflections* (New York: Random House, 1965), 325–26.

_____, in Hillman, James, *The Soul's Code: In Search of Character and Calling* (New York: Random House, 1996), x.

Kegan, *In Over Our Heads*, 179.

Kristof, Nicholas, "The Encore," reprinted from the *New York Times* in the *Winston-Salem Journal*, July 23, 2008, A–9.

Levinson, *The Seasons of a Man's Life*, 62–63, 251.

Rodriguez, Andres, *The Book of the Heart: The Poetics, Letters and Life of John Keats* (Hudson, NY: Lindisfarne Press, 1993), 48.

Shaw, George Bernard, *Man and Superman*, Act IV.

Sheehy, *New Passages,* 169.

_____, *Understanding Men's Passages: Discovering the New Map of Men's Lives* (New York: Random House, 1998), 99.

Tolstoy, Leo, in William James, *The Varieties of Religious Experience* (New York: Random House, 1961), 150–51.

Winston-Salem Journal. "In Service: Native of city discovered his life's mission in a changing South Africa," August 17, 2008, B–1, 3.

Choices I

Godin, Seth, *The Dip* (New York: Penguin, 2007), 51, 69.

Gould, Roger L., *Transformations: Growth and Change in Adult Life* (New York: Simon and Schuster, 1978), 244.

Handy, *Waiting for the Mountain to Move*, XXVI.

Hogan assessment instrumentation and information thereon may be found at www.hoganassessments.com.

Jung, *The Archetypes and the Collective Unconscious* (Princeton, NJ: Princeton University Press, 1959) 167.

_____, *The Structure and Dynamics of the Psyche*, 389.

_____, *Psychological Types* (Princeton, NJ: Princeton University Press, 1974), 456–57.

Kegan, Robert and Lahey, Lisa Laskow, "The Real Reason People Won't Change," (Harvard Business Review, Nov. 2001), 85–92.

Levinson, *The Seasons of a Man's Life*, 331.

O'Connor, Peter, *Understanding the Midlife Crisis* (New York: Paulist Press, 1981).

Roosevelt, Theodore, in *The Associated Press*, "Thought for Today," 10/27/08.

Sheehy, Gail, *Passages: Predictable Crises of Adult Life* (New York: Bantam, 1976), 409.

Stein, Murray and Hollwitz, John, eds., *Psyche at Work: Workplace Applications of Jungian Analytical Psychology* (Willmette, IL: Chiron Publications, 1992), 10–11.

Choices II

Glasser, William, *Control Theory: A New Theory of How We Control Our Lives* (New York: Harper and Row, 1985). The author expresses his appreciation to J. Anderson Little of Mediation, Inc., Chapel Hill, NC, for his insights into Glasser's work and the "Glasser Questions."

Gould, *Transformations*, 267, 288.

Hillman, *The Soul's Code*, 142.

Johnson, Robert A., *We: Understanding the Psychology of Romantic Love* (San Francisco: Harper & Row, 1983), 52, 103, 112.

_____, *Living Your Unlived Life*, 35.

_____ and Ruhl, Jerry M., *Contentment: A Way to True Happiness* (San Francisco: Harper San Francisco, 1999).

Jung, *The Development of Personality* (Princeton, NJ: Princeton University Press, 1954), 194–201. Throughout this passage, the "container" is cast in the masculine, the "contained" in the feminine. However, as the translator's note makes clear (195), this is "due entirely to the exigencies of English grammar, and is not implied in the German text. Needless to say, the situation could easily be reversed."

Kegan, *The Evolving Self*, 215, 218.

Von Franz, Marie-Louise, *Projection and Re-collection in Jungian Psychology* (LaSalle, IN: Open Court Publications, 1980).

Mistakes

Campbell, Joseph, *The Hero With a Thousand Faces* (Princeton, NJ: Princeton University Press, 1968), 51.

Edinger, Edward F., *The Aion Lectures* (Toronto: Inner City Books, 1996), 63–64.

_____, *The Creation of Consciousness: Jung's Myth for Modern Man* (Toronto: Inner City Books, 1984), 68.

Jaffe, Lawrence W., *Liberating the Heart: Spirituality and Jungian Psychology* (Toronto: Inner City Books, 1990), 17.

Jung, *Memories, Dreams, Reflections*, 297.

Palmer, *Let Your Life Speak*, 7, 99.

Quinn, *Deep Change*, 20–22.

Sheehy, *Passages*, 412, 513.

Propellers and Sandbars

Eliot, T. S., *The Cocktail Party*, in *T.S. Eliot: The Complete Poems and Plays 1909–1950* (New York: Harcourt Brace, 1980), 348.

Gould, *Transformations*, 243.

Greene, Graham, *A Burnt-Out Case* (New York: Viking Press, 1961), 240.

Hillman, *The Soul's Code*.

Hollis, *The Middle Passage*, 78.

James, William, as quoted in Awbrey, David S., *Finding Hope in the Age of Melancholy* (Boston: Little, Brown and Company, 1999), 159.

Johnson, Robert A., *Femininity Lost and Regained* (New York: Harper & Row, 1990), 92.

————, *Balancing Heaven and Earth: A Memoir* (San Francisco: Harper San Francisco, 1998), 103.

————, *Living Your Unlived Life*, 202.

Johnson and Ruhl, *Contentment*, 54.

Jung, *The Development of Personality* (Princeton, NJ: Princeton University Press, 1964), 173.

————, *Psychology and Religion: West and East* (Princeton, NJ: Princeton University Press, 1958), 330–31.

————, *The Structure and Dynamics of the Psyche*, 185, 395.

————, "Synchronicity: An Acausal Connecting Principle," in *The Structure and Dynamics of the Psyche*, 417–519.

Kaplan, *Beyond Ambition*, 176–77.

Kegan, *In over Our Heads*, 354.

Sanford, John A., ed., *Fritz Kunkel: Selected Writings* (New York: Paulist Press, 1984), 141.

Shakespeare, William, *Julius Caesar*, Act I, Scene ii.

Thompson, *The Congruent Life*, 249–253.

Safe Home

Campbell, *The Hero with a Thousand Faces*.

Confucius, *The Analects of Confucius*, translation by Arthur Waley (New York: Vintage Books, 1938), Book II, 88.

Eliot, *Four Quartets*, 54.

Erikson, *Identity and the Life Cycle*, 104–105.

Gould, *Transformations*, 318.

Helgoe, Laurie, "Revenge of the Introvert," in *Psychology Today*, Sept/Oct 2010, 54–61.

Jung, *Psychology and Religion: West and East*, 334.

_____, *The Structure and Dynamics of the Psyche*, 224, 226, 356, 400.

_____, *The Archetypes and the Collective Unconscious*, 167–168.

_____, *Memories, Dreams, and Reflections*, 335.

_____, *Psychological Types*, 105.

_____, *Two Essays on Analytical Psychology*, 173, 238.

Maxwell, Florida Scott, at www.famousquotesandauthors.com/ authors/florida_scott_maxwell_quotes.html.

Perlman, Medora Scoll, "Toward a Theory of the Self in the Group," in Stein and Hollwitz, eds., *Psyche at Work*, 181.

Studzinski, Raymond, *Spiritual Direction and Midlife Development* (Chicago: Loyola University Press, 1985), 62.

Thompson, *The Congruent Life*, 30–47.

Your Next Chapter

Claudia drew her inspiration for this conversation from Portia Nelson, *There's a Hole in My Sidewalk* (Hillsboro, Oregon: Beyond Words Publishing, 1993).

About the Author

MICHAEL THOMPSON IS AN attorney, management consultant, writer, and executive coach. His consulting practice has allowed him to work with hundreds of senior managers, executives, and teams on four continents. He is currently the president of RiverBlue Consulting, LLC. Prior to founding his own firm, he taught on the adjunct faculties of Duke Corporate Education, Inc. and The Center for Creative Leadership.

Michael is also a licensed attorney and a certified legal mediator. In addition to his private law practice, he was for eight years vice president and senior counsel of The Wachovia Corporation and taught for seven years at Wake Forest University's School of Business, where he also served as assistant dean.

His first book, *The Congruent Life: Following the Inward Path to Fulfilling Work and Inspired Leadership,* is published by Jossey-Bass and was nominated as one of the top ten business books of 2000. He also enjoys writing historical fiction, with his award-winning screenplay "Coldwater" now under option with Maurice Davis Films.

Michael earned his BA and Juris Doctor at the University of North Carolina and studied for two years at Washington's Shalem Institute for Spiritual Formation.

Michael Thompson and his wife, Jane, make their home in Winston-Salem and Sunset Beach, North Carolina. They have two grown daughters. He can be reached by e-mail at cmtwsnc@aol.com.

29794093R00113

Made in the USA
Lexington, KY
07 February 2014